Galatians
and
Ephesians

by Earl S. Johnson, Jr.

Table of Contents

Outline of Galatians and Ephesians

Galatians

I. Greetings (1:1-5)

II. Why the Letter Was Written (1:6-9)
   A. Turning to another gospel (1:6-7)
   B. There is only one gospel (1:8-9)

III. Paul's Gospel Is Valid (1:10–2:21)
   A. Paul's gospel comes directly from God (1:10-12)
   B. Paul is called to be an apostle (1:13-24)
   C. The Jerusalem conference (2:1-21)
      1. Must all Christians be circumcised? (2:1-6)
      2. Establishment of two ministries (2:7-10)
      3. Paul's run-in with Peter (2:11-21)

IV. Justification by Faith (3:1–4:31)
   A. Have you really understood the gospel? (3:1-5)
   B. Learn from examples from Scripture (3:6–4:31)
      1. The example of Abraham (3:6-9)
      2. Rescue from the curse of the law (3:10-14)
      3. God gives a covenant and a promise (3:15-21)
      4. The Law as tutor (3:22–4:7)
      5. Do not go back to slavery (4:8-20)
      6. Allegory of the two children (4:21-31)

V. The Gospel Makes Us Free (5:1-24)
   A. Christ has set us free (5:1)
   B. Through love, faith liberates us (5:2-6)
   C. An angry aside (5:7-12)
   D. Love calls us to serve one another (5:13-15)
   E. The law of the Spirit (5:16-25)

VI. Some Practical Examples (6:1-10)

VII. Conclusion (6:11-18)

Ephesians

I. Greetings (1:1-2)

II. God's Action in Christ (1:3-14)
    A. Blessed by God (1:3-4)
    B. Redeemed through Christ (1:7-8)
    C. United in Christ (1:9-12)
    D. Given the guarantee of the Spirit (1:13-14)

III. Giving Some Prayers of Thanksgiving (1:15-23)
    A. Thanks for your faith (1:15-18)
    B. Thanks for what God has done (1:19-23)

IV. Being Made Alive in Christ (2:1-10)
    A. Delivered from death (2:1-3)
    B. Made alive together in Christ (2:4-7)
    C. Saved by faith (2:8-10)

V. Building the One Household of Faith (2:11-22)
    A. You were once refugees of faith (2:11-12)
    B. Now you have peace with him (2:13-18)
    C. Unity in the household of God (2:19-22)

VI. Proclaiming the Mystery of Christ (3:1-13)

VII. Strengthening the Inner Person (3:14-21)
    A. Empowered internally by the Spirit (3:14-16)
    B. The dimensions of faith (3:17-19)
    C. A benediction (3:20-21)

VIII. Living The Moral Christian Life (4:1–6:17)
    A. Lead a worthy life (4:1-3)
    B. The unity of the body of Christ (4:4-16)
    C. The old nature and the new (4:17–5:20)
        1. Do not live as the Gentiles do! (4:17-19)
        2. Be renewed in the Spirit (4:20-24)
        3. Some practical examples (4:25–5:20)
    D. Obey the rules of the house (5:21–6:9)
        1. Husbands and wives (5:21-33)
        2. Children and parents (6:1-4)
        3. Slaves and masters (6:5-9)
    E. Put on the whole armor of God (6:10-17)

IX. Conclusion (6:18-24)

Introduction to Galatians

The Nature of the Epistle

Galatians presents one of the most spiritually vibrant and concise introductions to the Christian faith in the New Testament. In only a few chapters Paul brings readers examples of his most mature thought. Galatians opens with his defense of his apostleship (1:11–2:10) and his vision for the Gentile mission (2:11-18). Moving to his mystical understanding of being *crucified with Christ* and living *in Christ* (2:19-21), he then concentrates on his central concept of justification by faith (3:1–4:28) and the revelation that there is neither Jew nor Greek, male nor female, slave nor free since all are one in Christ (3:26-29). He completes the epistle with a moving definition of Christian freedom and the role of the Holy Spirit in daily life (5:1–6:16).

In Galatians Paul reveals his passionate concern for the truth of the gospel and the spiritual health of the congregations in Galatia. Skipping over his customary words of praise to a church community (see the "thanksgiving" sections in Romans 1:8-15; 1 Thessalonians 1:2-10; 2 Thessalonians 1:3-4; Philippians 1:3-11), he bluntly goes right to the heart of the problem. He begins the very first chapter with a strong reprimand: *I am astonished that you are so quickly deserting him* (1:6), and continues throughout the epistle to express his feelings openly. He condemns those who oppose his ministry (1:8-9), sarcastically hopes that those who favor circumcision will slip and cut themselves (5:12), defends his own ministry against all critics (1:11–2:21), uses personal examples to persuade his readers (2:20; 4:12-14; 4:19-20; 6:11), and ends with a testy challenge to his enemies to leave him (and the Galatians) alone in the future (6:17).

Recent research indicates that Galatians is partially modeled on a type of ancient Greek literature known as an *apologetic letter* which can be traced back at least to the fourth century B.C. In the ancient world an "apology" was not a personal request for forgiveness, but a formal defense in which an author argues against opponents in a fairly predictable form. Paul probably read numerous examples when he studied in Jerusalem (Acts 22:3). Throughout Galatians the outline of such a form is clearly visible: the introduction (1:6-11), the statement of the facts (1:12–2:14), the major proposition (2:15-21), the proofs (3:1–4:31), and the giving of practical advice (5:16–6:10).

It is also possible to see in Galatians how much Paul was influenced by the training he received as a rabbi and a Pharisee. In Galatians he admits rather proudly that he was first in his class in rabbinic studies: *I advanced in Judaism beyond many of my own age among my people* (1:14). In Acts 22:3 Luke records a speech in which Paul relates that he studied under the famous teacher Gamaliel and was *educated according to the strict manner of the law of our fathers*. In Chapters 3 and 4 of Galatians he employs arguments from Old Testament Scriptures which move in a kind of logic which was very common in the Judaism he studied in the first century but remains very foreign to modern readers today. Most of his first-century readers no doubt found his arguments very persuasive, however, and were motivated to accept his reasons for believing in Jesus as the Christ predicted in the Old Testament.

The Author

Although some of the New Testament books traditionally attributed to Paul were probably not written by him but were composed later by some of his followers (see the Introduction to Ephesians), Bible scholars generally agree that the apostle Paul is certainly the author of Galatians. The very first word in the text is his name, and the argument and style are similar to those in his other authentic letters, especially the much longer Epistle to the Romans. At the end of Galatians he admits that a secretary has actually transcribed the text, but he signs it with his own hand: *See with what large letters I am writing to you with my own hand* (6:11), so that no one will doubt that it is his.

The Galatians

Even though it is certain that the churches of Galatia (1:2) were located somewere in the general area known in the first century A.D. as Asia Minor (what is now modern Turkey), it is not possible to determine precisely where the people to whom Paul wrote were living. At various times in history the word *Galatia* referred to regions either in the central or the southern part of that area, and it is difficult to know how Paul defined the term. Scholars who think that the letter went to congregations in the Roman province in the south suppose that Paul visited them when he traveled to other nearby cities (Acts 13:14–14:23; 16:1–18:23), but it is impossible to be sure. References elsewhere in the New Testament provide very little concrete information about where Galatia was (Acts 16:6; 18:23; 1 Corinthians 16:1; 2 Timothy 4:10; 1 Peter 1:1). The itineraries given for Paul's travels in Acts are notoriously difficult to coordinate with the information provided in Galatians 1 and 2.

The Occasion

Wherever the Galatia was to which Paul wrote, it is clear that the reason why he corresponded with the Christians living there was that they were under severe pressure to abandon the message of faith that he had given to them on a previous visit (1:9; 4:13-20). The opponents with whom Paul is so angry were probably Jewish-Christian missionaries (possibly from Jerusalem, as

2:1-21 seems to imply) who came to Galatia after Paul founded the churches there. Their mission was to bring the Galatians' faith in line with a Christianity that still observed the major principles of the Torah and the traditions of Judaism. In Paul's view what they offered was not merely a fine-tuning but a perversion of the gospel of Christ, a second gospel which was not a gospel at all. The opponents taught a number of things that Paul rejected: that Christians still had to be circumcised to believe in Jesus Christ (2:1-6); that they had to depend on works of the law to be saved (3:1-4:28); and that they had to keep ritual observances of the Jewish calendar (4:10) in order to be true believers in God. Against this point of view, Paul argues that they must return to the true gospel which he originally taught them, that they must not exchange the truth for a lie (2:14) or trade their new-found freedom for slavery again (4:8-9). Instead they must believe in God's promise in Scripture, visible especially in the life of Abraham and fulfilled in Christ, so that they will live life by faith and faith alone.

The Date

Galatians was probably written during one of Paul's later missionary tours (see Acts 15:36–18:22; 18:24–21:17) between the years 50 and 55 A.D. It is likely that he composed it after he finished the letters to the church in Corinth and just before he began his longer epistle to the Romans. Although church tradition says that he wrote it while he was in the city of Ephesus (see 1 Corinthians 16:8; Acts 19:1-10), it is also possible that it could have been sent from Macedonia, Antioch, Corinth, or even Rome.

PART ONE

Galatians 1:1-5

Introduction to These Verses

Most of the information we have about Paul comes from the New Testament in the Acts of the Apostles and from his other letters. Unfortunately it is not possible to be certain that all of the references to him in Acts are historically accurate, since they do not always agree completely with what Paul writes about himself elsewhere. Thus is it necessary to be cautious when assembling information about his life. Galatians 1:1–2:21 presents difficulties for those who wish to compare this section with the description of Paul's ministry in the Acts of the Apostles. But the verses there still provide valuable information about the beginning of Paul's work as an apostle as he describes God's call to service, the independent establishment of his work, the important conference he had in Jerusalem with other apostles who were well-known in the church (*the pillars*, 2:9; also see Acts 15), and the critical debate he had with Peter over the matter of circumcision.

Greetings (1:1-5)

Paul begins his letter to the Galatians with his own name and a reference to the fact that he is an apostle appointed by Jesus Christ and God the Father. This is a normal way for him to start a letter (see Romans 1:1; 1 Corinthians 1:1; 2 Corinthians 1:1; Colossians 1:1), although he occasionally adds the title *servant* after his name as well (see Romans 1:1; Philippians 1:1).

Concerning Paul's name, Acts 13:9 reports that Paul was also called Saul, and up to that point in Luke's account he is called nothing else (Acts 9:1-22; 11:25, 30; 13:1-2; also see 22:7, 13). Saul was his Hebrew name and apparently Paul (a Greek spelling of the Roman surname *Paulos*) was his name in the Roman world, where Greek was the most common language.

In Galatians the word *apostle* is especially important because Paul is forced by his opponents to defend his calling as one who is sent by God to preach the good news of Jesus Christ. Apparently Paul's enemies argued that he did not preach the right message (1:6-9), and did not have the proper beginning in the faith (1:13-14) or the correct training to be called a true apostle (1:18-20). What was more, it was well known that at one time he had been a brutal persecutor of the church (1:13; Philippians 3:6). But Paul argues strongly that he is an apostle and that his calling has nothing to do with human standards of judgment, but comes directly from God (1:15-17) through Jesus Christ.

The word *apostle* literally means *one who is sent out*, and refers to a representative, an emissary, or a delegate. Such a person was often commissioned by a king or queen, for example, to represent the royal house in diplomatic negotiations. Although it is difficult to know precisely how people earned the right to use such a title in the early church, it appears that at the very least one had to have a direct commission from the risen Jesus and had to have certain gifts from the Holy Spirit to qualify (see Acts 1:1-26; 1 Corinthians 12:1-11, 29). Galatians and Romans make it clear that Paul was particularly sensitive about this point because his apostolic authority had been challenged. Thus he had to prove that he was a full-fledged apostle and that his commission did come directly from Jesus. He believed that he qualified on several counts.

Although he had not been present at the crucifixion or

the Resurrection and had persecuted the church ruthlessly for a time, he had received his commission from Jesus on the Damascus road through a special post-Resurrection appearance . This event obviously made a tremendous impact on his life and work (Acts 9:1-19; 22:3-11; Galatians 1:12).

God had given him a special position among the apostles. His calling was to be the apostle to the Gentiles and to the Jews living in Gentile areas (Acts 13:44-48; Galatians 2:7).

As he says in 2 Corinthians 12:11-13, he had performed the signs of a true apostle: *with signs and wonders and mighty works*.

Even though he had become an apostle after the first disciples and had come so late, in fact, that he could call himself an *afterbirth* or *miscarriage* of an apostle, he was still an apostle nevertheless (see 1 Corinthians 15:8-10).

§ § § § § § §

The Message of Galatians 1:1-5

§ Paul is an apostle of Jesus Christ, and thus he is entrusted with a special mission to preach the good news to others.

§ Paul's authority comes directly from God.

§ § § § § § §

PART TWO Galatians 1:6-9

Introduction to These Verses

Paul opens the second section of his letter with words of astonishment about the unfaithfulness of the Galatians to the truth of the gospel. What happened was this: After Paul had set up churches in the area of Galatia by his preaching and teaching of the message about Jesus Christ, Jewish-Christian missionaries came later and presented a different message. Apparently they, like Paul and many others, have been converted to Christianity from the Jewish faith. But, unlike Paul, they believe that one can continue to be a Jew in all ways and be a Christian, too, as if the Christian faith were merely tacked on to their earlier beliefs. Paul does not agree. For him the gospel is not an afterthought to Judaism. Although it is based on the Old Testament, it is a new revelation from God and it is distinct because it is based on Jesus Christ, his life, death, and resurrection.

Turning to Another Gospel (1:6-7)

Paul is surprised that the Galatians are actually turning to this different gospel. The word *gospel* means *good news*. In the New Testament it refers to the good news preached by Jesus that the kingdom of God is at hand (Mark 1:14-15). Paul uses it to describe early Christian preaching about Jesus (Romans 1:1-6; 1 Corinthians 15:1-8). It has been given by God, promised by the prophets, and it is about Jesus, his resurrection, and lifting up to glory in the father.

In the ancient world *gospel* was used in different ways. In the Old Testament the verb *to bring good news* refers to the message that the nation had won a victory (1 Samuel 31:9). Later the good news was the prophecy that Israel would be liberated from captivity (Isaiah 40:9; 41:27; 52:7). In the New Testament the same verb is found in Jesus' first sermon when he quotes Isaiah 61:1-2, *The Spirit of the Lord is upon me, because he has anointed me to preach the good news to the poor* (Luke 4:18). Paul uses it in Galatians 1:8 where it is translated *preach*. In Greek society the word *gospel* was also used in the proclamation of a military victory. Sometimes the news was sent by letter, sometimes by courier. It was "good news" because it meant the defeat of an enemy, more territory, the spoils of war, and a time of peace.

In Rome the word *gospel* often was given a political meaning and was used to describe messages about the emperor. Information about him was "good news" because Romans often considered emperors after Julius Caesar to be saviors, gods, or sons of a god. In a famous inscription about the birth of one of the emperors it was said that the birthday of the god was for the world *the beginning of the good messages which have gone forth because of him* (Priene inscription). The same word was used to describe the time when emperors took their thrones, because Romans looked forward joyfully to a new age, one which would be marked by peace for the whole world.

Paul's readers are no doubt aware of the background of the word *gospel* when he uses it in Galatians, and he builds on their understanding. For Paul, the gospel of Jesus Christ is the knowledge that Old Testament prophecies about future liberation are fulfilled in Jesus. What is more, Christians should believe that this "good news" is far more important than information about new developments in the Roman empire. In Jesus the promised kingdom of God, the real new age, is already at hand.

Deserting the True Gospel

In verse 6 Paul indicates how he knows that the Galatians are not following the truth of the gospel. They are deserting *him who called you in the grace of Christ*. In other words, they have abandoned their calling as Christians, they have not been true to Jesus, and they have accepted preaching and teaching which does not have grace (the gift of God in Christ) at its core. Grace is the key to the gospel, and any preaching or teaching that says that believers have to do anything more than believe in Jesus Christ to be put right with God is obviously false.

Verse 6 says that the Galatians are doing more than committing an error in judgment, or misunderstanding Paul's teaching. They are also abandoning their calling from God (*deserting him who called you*). For Paul the call is a very important concept. In the Old Testament special servants of God were given tasks by the direct summons of God. Examples are Abraham (Genesis 12:1-3), Moses (Exodus 2:7-10), and the prophets (Isaiah 6:8-9; Jeremiah 1:4-10). Paul uses the same word to indicate how he became an apostle (Galatians 1:15; Romans 1:1; 1 Corinthians 1:1). More importantly for Galatians 1, Paul believes that all Christians are called to believe in Christ and serve God (Romans 1:6). As he says in Romans 8:30, *and those whom he predestined he also called; and those whom he called he also justified; and those whom he justified he also glorified*. In 1 Corinthians 1:26 he directs his readers to *consider your call*, that is, how God chose as servants the poor rather than the rich, so no one could boast of his or her own work on God's behalf. For references to Jesus' call of the disciples see Mark 3:13-14 and John 10:3-18. By reminding the Galatians of their call, Paul hopes to help them remember how they became Christians in the first place and prevent them from falling under the influence of a "different" gospel.

Although the Revised Standard Version uses the word

deserting in verse 6, it is not part of Paul's original text. In that verse he only uses one Greek verb where the RSV uses two (*deserting, turning*). Literally, the verse can be translated, *I am astonished how quickly you are turning from your calling in the grace of Christ to another gospel.* The word *turning* means to change one's mind, turn away, or desert. In noun form it means *turncoat* and was often used in apologies (see the Introduction) to describe political traitors. The verb is used in Jude 4 to describe *ungodly persons who pervert the grace of our God into licentiousness and deny our only Master and Lord, Jesus Christ.*

Turning in verse 6 is similar to another verb in verse 7, *pervert (metastreph)*. It means *to alter, change, or misrepresent.* By using these two words beginning with the Greek letters *m-e-t-a*, Paul may be making a play on the Greek word for repentance (*metanoia*), which means a change of mind or a reversal of direction (see Mark 1:14-15; Romans 2:4; 2 Corinthians 7:9-10). When the Galatians became Christians, God had changed their lives and they had turned around to Christ. But now, sadly, they were turning to another gospel and altering the truth they had first learned. Instead of repenting and turning their lives around 180 degrees, they were turning 360 degrees and ending up right where they started. They needed to return to their original commitment to Jesus.

There Is Only One Gospel (1:8-9)

In verses 8-9 Paul tries to help the Galatians solve their spiritual problem. He writes about another gospel, one contrary to the message he first preached to the Galatians, which is leading them astray. The problem was not unique to the Galatians. New Testament writers often had to deal with Christian preaching which contradicted the truth of Christ. Paul argues against *superlative apostles* in 2 Corinthians 11:4-5 and 12:11, for example, who were misleading Christians in Corinth by preaching another

Jesus and a different spirit. In 2 Thessalonians 2:1-3 and 3:10-12 he warns believers against those who urge members of the church not to work because they claim to know when the world will come to an end. Other teachers in Philippi whom Paul calls *dogs* and *evil-workers* argue that Christians must keep the Old Testament law (Philippians 3:2). Other examples are found in 2 Timothy 2:16-18; 4:3-4; and Revelation 2:20. All of this sounds familiar to Christians of any age as pastors still argue with one another about the truth and the proper understanding of the Bible, and television preachers try to outdo each other with their revelations from God. Paul settles the matter in the Galatian churches by making it clear that even though people can preach false things about Christ, there really is no other gospel. The reason why the conference described in Galatians 2:1-10 was held was to take two gospels, the gospel to the uncircumcised and the gospel to the circumcised (2:7), and make them into one gospel of Christ. There is no other, because there is only one Christ and all Christians are one in him. Just as there cannot be Jew or Greek, male or female, or slave or free in Christ (3:28), so there cannot be more than one gospel. What Paul's opponents teach is not a gospel because it lacks the oneness of Christ, it lacks the grace of Christ (1:6), and it lacks the freedom (5:1) that Christ brings. In short, it is not a gospel because it lacks Christ himself.

The word *angel* in verse 8 indicates that the Galatians should not accept the message of anyone who teaches anything different from that which Paul has already taught. *Angel* means *messenger*. Angels are heavenly beings who serve God and carry God's messages. They are often mentioned in Old Testament accounts as they warn people and help them (Genesis 16:7-14; 19:1-22; 22:11, 15-18; Exodus 3:2; 23:20-23; 2 Kings 19:35). In the New Testament they bring messages about Jesus' birth (Matthew 1:20; Luke 1:11-38) and his resurrection

(Matthew 28:2-7; Mark 16:5; Luke 24:4). Paul says that even if it appears that a spiritual being is bringing a gospel different from his own, the Galatians should not believe it. He is able to say this, not because he is so vain that he thinks that only he knows the truth, but because he has received his gospel directly from Jesus. Since it is from the risen Lord, it is impossible that a true angel could contradict it, since an angel would be under Christ's command, and Christ could not contradict himself.

Paul ends this section with a curse (verses 8 and 9) on those who teach a gospel other than the one that Christ brings. The Greek word for *accursed* is *anathema*, and it is still used in English today. An anathema is a person who is detested or loathed, one who is condemned to God's punishment. Paul uses the same word to end 1 Corinthians (16:22) when he writes, *If anyone has no love for the Lord, let him be accursed*. While it is possible that he makes some kind of a magical association with the word as if he were casting some kind of mysterious voodoo on his opponents, it is more likely that it is in line with the kinds of curses enemies receive in the Old Testament, especially in the cursing psalms. Psalm 137:8-9 and Malachi 2:2 are prime examples. In Galatians Paul says that those who oppose Christ will get what they deserve. They will be cut off from him (5:4) and will not receive the grace and peace which only he can give (1:3).

§ § § § § § § §

The Message of Galatians 1:6-9

§ Paul is astonished that the Galatians are deserting the grace of Christ and turning to another gospel. There are those who are troubling the Galatians and perverting the good news of Jesus Christ. Paul argues that there really is not another gospel, since just as Christ is one, all teaching that comes from him is also one. No one, not even an angel, can preach a gospel that is contrary to Paul's, because Paul's gospel was given to him by the risen Jesus himself. Those who do such a thing will be cursed and condemned, because by distorting the truth they have cut themselves off from God the Father and from the grace and peace of Jesus Christ.

§ § § § § § § §

PART THREE Galatians 1:10–2:6

Introduction to These Chapters

The third section of Galatians begins Paul's statement of the facts in the defense of his ministry. In basic outline the facts are: His ministry is God's will, not just his own; he learned the gospel from God, not from others; God has changed his life; God prepared him in Arabia; the other apostles accepted his ministry; he now lives in Christ and Christ lives in him.

Paul's Gospel Comes From God (1:10-12)

In verses 10-11 Paul asks his readers two rhetorical questions. Am I trying to please other people? The answer is "No!" I am not trying to impress other Christians. My gospel is God's. It is not a human gospel. Am I trying to please God? The answer is "Yes!" I am a servant of God. In these verses Paul struggles with a harsh reality that all Christians must often face: It is not always possible to please God and the people around you at the same time. In Galatians 1:10-11 Paul insists that he has not made the mistake of trying to express a purely human opinion that would be pleasing to other people and easy for them to understand, so that his message could be more popular. All he wants to do is please God and preach the truth about Christ. Paul also makes it clear that he will not resort to trickery, slick talk, or hocus-pocus to get people to listen to his gospel. Seeking the favor of his readers or listeners or pleasing people are both references to practices some preachers and philosophers used in the ancient world to attract audiences. Paul indicates that he will not use magic or religious quackery to communicate God's message. Those who do so are hucksters of the gospel who use flattery or preach out of greed (1 Thessalonians 2:5-6), those who only offer *eyeservice* to the church (Ephesians 6:6), those who do not sincerely seek the things that are above (Colossians 3:2).

What is Paul if he is not a people pleaser? He is a servant of Christ (see Colossians 3:23-24). In Greek the word *servant* is *doulos* and can also mean *slave*. Paul uses it in reference to himself in the opening words of Romans and Thessalonians. Furthermore, he indicates in Romans 6:16-19, that, in his opinion, human beings have no choice but to be slaves to some passion, cause, or point of view. Everyone is subject to an emperor, king, employer, or owner. Part of human sin is being subject to everything or anything but the will of God in Christ. Paul thanks God in Romans that the Christian has been freed from slavery to sin and can now be a slave to something positive, a slave to righteousness. The Christian, through Christ, exchanges a negative addiction for a positive one, and is now a slave and a servant of Christ. (See the discussions of slavery in 3:28 and Ephesians 6:5-9.)

When Paul says that he is a slave of Christ, however, he has even more in mind. In the Old Testament, leaders whom God chose for his people are often called *servants* (Exodus 32:13; Deuteronomy 34:5; Judges 2:8; 1 Samuel 3:9; 2 Samuel 7:5; 1 Kings 3:7; 2 Kings 14:25; Job 1:8). In familiar passages in Isaiah (42:1-4; 49:1-6; 50:4-9; 52:13–53:12) the prophet speaks passionately about the messiah who will not be a mighty king, but a suffering servant of the Lord. In the New Testament Jesus presents himself as a servant (John 13:1-20) and teaches the disciples that they must serve others, too (Mark 9:35; 10:42-45). As Paul says in Philippians 2:5-11, Christians believe that Jesus set the example by humbling himself,

GALATIANS AND EPHESIANS

giving up his divine privileges as the Son of God and becoming a servant, being born as a human being. When Paul says he is a servant, he sees himself in this humble tradition, most perfectly represented by the suffering and death of Jesus himself.

In verse 12 Paul reasserts what he has already said in 1:1: His gospel did not come from any human being but only from Christ himself. When he says that he did not receive the gospel from others, he distinguishes himself from his readers, who had no choice but to receive it from Paul (1:8-9, 11; 3:1-2; 4:13-14). But Paul is different from his readers. He is an apostle, and they are not. Even though he was willing to check out what he had learned from Christ with the other apostles (1:18-24; 2:2), he had all the knowledge and doctrine he needed before he met them, and they added nothing to him (2:6).

How did he learn about the gospel, then? Paul says it was through revelation. *Revelation* means the uncovering of something which is true, the unveiling of a mystery about God or God's will for humanity. In the Bible revelation sometimes comes through visions (Isaiah 6:1-13; Jeremiah 1:11-13), special signs such as the burning bush (Exodus 3:2-4), or through special messengers sent by God (Genesis 18:1–19:1). In 1 Corinthians Paul indicates that he received basic information about Jesus' death and resurrection through an appearance by the risen Jesus to him personally (15:8). Probably this is the same experience described in Acts 9:1-9, although it is not absolutely certain. Paul indicates in Galatians 1:17 that God instructed him in Arabia as well.

Paul Is Called to Be an Apostle (1:13-24)

Paul moves from the brief description of how he learned the gospel to what he learned and did before he became a Christian. Verses 13-17 are very important to Paul in his defense of his ministry. Because the Galatians already know about the atrocities he has committed (*for you have heard*, verse 13), he has to be honest and open about what he was, how he has changed, and what he is now. He mentions his former life in Judaism because he wants to make clear how much he has changed. He has come a long way since the days when he was a Pharisee, and his life is totally different now that it is in Christ.

Generally, Paul gives very little information about his past in his letters. In 1 Corinthians 15:9 he admits that he has persecuted the church. In Philippians 3:5-6 he gives a brief summary of salient facts: He was circumcised as a baby on the eighth day, according the Jewish custom; he belonged to the tribe of Benjamin; he was trained as a Pharisee (see the discussion of 1:15 below); he was a persecutor of the church; he kept the Jewish law fully.

The only information available about what Paul means by the words *I persecuted the church of God violently and tried to destroy it* in Galatians 1:13 comes from the Book of Acts. Acts 7:58 says that Paul was present at Stephen's murder and indicates that he took part in it (8:1). Acts 9:1 says that he was *breathing threats and murder against the disciples of the Lord* and asked for warrants from the high priest so he could take an expedition to arrest Christians wherever he could find them. Luke reports the words of Paul's formal defense before Agrippa in Acts 26, where Paul says that he not only shut Christians in prison, but put many to death, admitting, *I cast my vote against them* (26:10). Although some biblical scholars question the reliability of these verses, Acts provides some idea of Paul's reputation (Galatians 1:23) and why it was so necessary for him to prove to the Galatians that he was no longer an enemy, but a friend in Christ.

In verses 13-14 Paul discusses his own religious background. By *Judaism* he means the Jewish religion as distinct from the Christian faith or any other religion. Judaism was a belief system based on the Old Testament law, the teaching of the prophets, the worship required in the first five books of the Old Testament, and the traditions of the fathers, that is, later interpretations of the Old Testament teachings. In Judaism the teachings of the fathers—the teaching of the rabbis and scribes—was received by Jews with great reverence and respect, and in synagogue services today such traditions are frequently quoted in sermons and liturgical readings.

In verse 14 Paul asserts rather boastfully that he was a superior student. When he says that he *advanced in Judaism beyond many of my own age among my people* and that he was *zealous,* he means that he studied hard, was committed to what he learned, and became a Jewish leader. Acts 22:3 reports that he studied under Gamaliel, one of the most famous rabbis. In Philippians 3:5 he says that he became a Pharisee. The Pharisees made up a group of Jews who studied the law very carefully and tried to live it as completely as possible. They believed in ritual, purity, tithing, religious piety, and Jewish separateness from the Romans and other Gentiles. In the New Testament they are usually characterized as the ones who were the most opposed to Jesus (Matthew 23; Mark 7:1-13). The Pharisees were experts in the Jewish law and believed that it was a primary source of truth about God (see Psalm 119). It was a belief that Paul rejected when he became a Christian and one that he will tirelessly argue against throughout the rest of Galatians.

The expression *set me apart before I was born* in verse 15 refers to Paul's belief that God had planned to call him as an apostle to the Gentiles from the time he was conceived. His calling (see the discussion on 1:6) was not a matter of fate, luck, or his own choice, but part of God's plan for Paul's life and for the church of Christ. To *set apart* means to make holy, that is, make special for use in God's service. (See Acts 13:2; Romans 1:1.) The Greek word for *set apart* is *aphoriz,* and Paul may be using it to make a play on the word *Pharisee.* Some scholars argue that the word *Pharisee* comes from a Hebrew verb, *pharash,* which means *to distinguish, separate.* If this is true,

Paul may be saying, "God once separated me to be a 'separated one' (*Pharisee*), but now he has set me apart (*aphoriz*) to be a servant of Christ." *Before I was born* points to the belief that God determines the destiny of those who are called from the beginning of their lives. As God did it for some prophets (1 Samuel 1–3; Jeremiah 1:5), for John the Baptist (Luke 1:5-24), and for Jesus (Matthew 1:18-25; Luke 1:26-56; Colossians 1:15-20), so God did it for Paul.

The word *grace* is discussed in reference to 1:3. *Gentiles* in verse 16 refers to all people who are not Jews. The English word, *Gentile*, comes from the Latin *gens*, meaning *nation*. Paul believes that God has separated and called him to preach the good news to the people who are not Jewish by birth (see 1:9). In the Old Testament a strict separation is maintained between Jew and Gentile in regard to beliefs, marriage, and international affairs (Exodus 23:28-33; Deuteronomy 7:1-5; Joshua 23:4-13). The prophets often predicted, however, that a time would come when Israel would be a light to the nations (Isaiah 42:6; 60:3), and the Gentiles would come to Jerusalem to learn the Jewish law (Isaiah 2–4). In Romans 10:12-21 Paul declares that in Christ the time has now come when the distinction will be removed between Jew and Gentile, for *every one who calls on the name of the Lord will be saved* (10:13). There he sees the irony of the gospel: The Jews who bring the good news, by having Christ come from them, may be, because of their rebellion against God, the last to realize its benefits.

When Paul says that he *did not confer with flesh and blood* in verse 16, he simply means that he did not discuss with anyone, any human being, what he should do or preach (see 1 Corinthians 15:3, 8). Verse 17 reiterates and expands what already has been said in the previous verse. Paul did not speak to anyone about his experience. He did not go to Jerusalem, the holy city of the Jews, to present himself to the other apostles, but went immediately into Arabia. Jerusalem was important as the capital of the Jewish state, the holy city of David and the place where Jesus died and was raised. It was also important to Paul and the Galatians, moreover, because it was the headquarters of the Christian church at the time (see 2:1-10). It was also from Jerusalem that the false brethren who were trying to undermine Paul's gospel were getting their support and backing (2:4).

Paul says in verse 17 that he went immediately into Arabia after he met Jesus on the Damascus road. This verse is one of those that presents historians with problems when they try to compare Galatians and Acts, since Acts 9:26-29 and 26:19-20 give very different itineraries. Arabia is not the large desert peninsula south and west of Jerusalem, but the area east of Damascus. Possibly Paul went there to meditate and learn from God, as prophets had before him (1 Kings 19:4; Mark 1:4, 13). Damascus (see Acts 9:1-9) was the city Paul visited immediately after he encountered the risen Lord. It was there that he first heard the good news of Jesus Christ, and there that he began to preach. Galatians 1:17 says that he returned there after his visit to Arabia. Damascus is the capital of Syria and was a major city in Paul's day.

Those who were apostles before me in verse 17 refers to Christians who had been called by God to exercise authority in the church as apostles before Paul received his call. (See the discussion of *apostle* in reference to 1:1). It is not possible to know who all of them were, but they certainly included James, Peter, John, and Barnabas (Galatians 1:18; 2:9; Acts 9:27), and possibly other disciples of Jesus.

Paul says in verse 18 that he *went up to Jerusalem* to visit Cephas and stay with him for fifteen days. *Cephas* is the Aramaic name for the apostle Peter. Paul uses that name in 1:18; 2:9, 11, and 14, whereas *Peter* appears in 2:7-8. *Cephas* means *rock* in Aramaic and *Peter* means the same in Greek. According to the Gospels, Peter was the spokesman for the disciples and had his name changed by Jesus from Simon (Matthew 16:16-19; John 1:35-42). He plays a leading role in the gospel story (see Mark 8:29-30; 9:2; 14:26-72; John 20:1-10; 21:15-23) and in Acts (2:14-42; 3:1-26; 10:32-48). Paul says in Galatians 2:8 that Peter was entrusted by God with the mission to the circumcised. According to tradition, he was persecuted and died as a Christian martyr in Rome (John 21:18-19; 1 Peter 5:1; 2 Peter 1:14).

Paul mentions in verse 20 that he also saw James, the brother of Jesus. Mark 6:3 lists James as one of Jesus' brothers, and although he was not a disciple during Jesus' lifetime (Mark 3:31-35; John 7:3-5), he became a leading figure in Jerusalem after Jesus' resurrection (Acts 1:14; 15:13; 21:18). Most scholars assume that after Peter left on his missionary tours, James became the head of the Jerusalem church (Acts 12:17). Paul mentions his name along with those of Cephas and John (Galatians 2:9) to show that the only apostles he conferred with were those who were leaders in the church. Paul adds a solemn oath in verse 20 to assure his readers that he is telling the truth that he saw no one else (*before God I do not lie!*). But it is difficult to reconcile that statement with the list of people Luke says that Paul visited in Acts 9:26-31. Perhaps Paul simply means in Galatians that those were the only leaders he met with at that time.

Syria (verse 21) is the name for the nation which surrounded Damascus. Cilicia is the name of a Roman province in southwestern Asia Minor (Turkey), just north of Syria. Paul's hometown of Tarsus (Acts 21:39) was one of its leading cities. Paul visited it on at least one other occasion (Acts 15:40-41). Judea (verse 22) is the name of the area in southern Palestine around Jerusalem.

The Jerusalem Conference (2:1-21)

Galatians 2 begins with Paul's statement that fourteen years later he went up to Jerusalem with Barnabas. The fourteen years are probably calculated from the time of the Damascus road experience, although they may refer to the period which began after his first visit to Cilicia (1:21). During that time Paul must have been engaged in the first of his missionary tours (Acts 13–14).

The reason Paul went to Jerusalem was to attend a conference with James, Cephas, and John (2:9) to decide the future direction of the Christian mission. The main issue was circumcision (2:3, 7, 9). Circumcision is the surgical removal of the foreskin of the penis, a religious rite practiced by Jews on the eighth day after a boy's birth (see Luke 1:59; Philippians 3:5). It is still practiced by Jews today and is a joyous celebration called a *brist*. According to Genesis 17:11-12, God ordered Abraham to institute the practice as a sign of the everlasting covenant with the people. Originally circumcision may have been started to ward off evil, or possibly for health reasons. But even though other nations practiced it (Jeremiah 9:25-26), Israel saw it as a spiritual act which showed the closeness of God to the chosen people.

The problem that developed in the early church was that since the first Christians were all Jews, just as Jesus was a Jew, they assumed that Christians would follow Jewish practices as part of their new faith, and they circumcised their children as a matter of course. Paul and others saw the matter differently. Most of their work was with non-Jews who had never adopted the custom. The matter came to a head when Paul refused to have a recent convert, Titus, circumcised (2:3, 5) because he was a Greek, not a Jew. As Paul explains in Galatians 3 and 4 and also in Romans 3 and 4, circumcision was more important as a symbol of faith than as a literal enactment of that faith. As he writes in Romans 2:28-29, *For he is not a real Jew who is one outwardly, nor is true circumcision something external and physical. He is a Jew who is one inwardly, and real circumcision is a matter of the heart, spiritual and not literal.* Paul's opinion was supported by many writers of the Old Testament (Leviticus 26:41; Deuteronomy 10:16; 30:6; Jeremiah 4:4; 6:10, Revised Standard Version note *h*; Ezekiel 44:7, 9; see Philippians 3:3).

Galatians 2:4 indicates that false brethren tried to disrupt Paul's ministry by attempting to force people who had become Christians under his preaching to be circumcised. At the conference in Jerusalem it was decided that Paul's point of view was absolutely correct and that he could continue his ministry unchanged. Acts 15:1-29 appears to report the same meeting, although it differs from the account in Galatians 2 in some details.

Barnabas (2:1) was an apostle and a leading Christian missionary. (See Acts 4:36-37; 9:27; 11:22.) Although he accompanied Paul on his first missionary tour (Acts 13), they had a disagreement about John Mark and never worked together again (Acts 15:36-41). Paul mentions somewhat sadly in Galatians 2:13 that Barnabas was sometimes sympathetic to those who tried to continue Jewish traditions in the church.

Titus (2:1) was Greek and probably one of Paul's protoges. According to 2 Corinthians 2:13; 7:6, 13-14; 8:6, 16, 23; 12:18, he was the organizer of the collection for Jerusalem. Tradition says that the New Testament letter of Titus was written to him.

Galatians 2:2 presents another historical difficulty for those who wish to reconcile Galatians 2 with Acts 15. Although Paul says that he went up to Jerusalem by revelation (see the commentary on 1:12), Acts 15:2 reports that he and Barnabas were appointed to go there by the Christians in Antioch. Paul may simply mean that he was not forced by pressure from the pillars in Jerusalem to attend a conference with them. But it is strange that in Galatians he insists so strongly on his independence, whereas in Acts Luke says in a rather commonplace way that the strategy was laid out by other people.

The second half of verse 2 (*I laid before them the gospel*

which I preach among the Gentiles) seems to indicate that
Paul outlined the basic message of his teaching and
preaching to see if it was the same one apostles in
Jerusalem were preaching. Clearly he did not do so to
seek their approval, as if he were a candidate for
ordination. He was already convinced of the truth of his
gospel (1:6-17), and he went mainly to make sure that the
church was one in Christ in its message and purpose.

Those who were of repute (2:2, 6, 9) refers to those who
were the leaders of the church in Jerusalem. This
expression appears elsewhere in the New Testament only
in Mark 10:42, where Jesus uses it in a negative way to
describe rulers who *are supposed to rule over the Gentiles and
lord it over them*. Scholars disagree whether Paul uses it in
a negative or a positive sense in Galatians. It is difficult to
decide. Even though he indicates that he has respect for
James, Cephas, and John, he also makes it clear that he
considers himself to be at least their equal. He
emphasizes his superior religious background (1:14), the
uniqueness of his calling (1:15-16), and the fact that he
had not consulted them previously about what he should
do or preach (1:18-19). He also states in 2:6 that they
added nothing whatsoever to him. *Those who were of repute*
is similar to the word *pillars* in 2:9. *Pillars* is not used this
way elsewhere in the New Testament, but in other
Christian literature it refers to respected Christian leaders
(1 Clement 5:2). The Revised Standard Version
translation, *who were reputed to be pillars*, implies that there
is some doubt in Paul's mind that they are all that sturdy
as supporters of the church. Probably he recognizes that
James, Cephas, and John are peers in ministry, even
though he is also aware of their faults, as 2:11-14 clearly
points out.

Lest somehow I should be running or had run in vain (2:2)
does not refer to Paul's concern that his gospel might have
been incorrect or ineffective. His concern instead is to make
sure that the apostles in Jerusalem not jeopardize his work

among the Gentiles by imposing Jewish restrictions on Christian freedom. Athletic competitions were very common in Greek society, and Paul often uses images from track and field events as symbols of the Christian life (1 Corinthians 9:24; Philippians 2:16; 2 Thessalonians 3:1). After all the training Paul has gone through, and considering the importance of the gospel, Paul wants to make sure that the truth is not edged out at the finish line by false brothers who sneak in (2:4) at the last minute, or so-called "pillars" who are wishy-washy in the faith (2:11-14).

The *false* or pseudo *brethren* in 2:4 are probably Jewish-Christian believers from Jerusalem who had come to the Galatian churches after Paul had preached there, and were trying to get the Galatians to adhere to Jewish practices. He uses the same term in 2 Corinthians 11:26 to describe those who endanger his mission. *Secretly brought in* implies that the opposition smuggled them into Galatia without Paul's knowledge, as if they were some kind of religious contraband or secret agents being brought over the border. Their aim is to spy out the Galatians' freedom and bring them back into slavery to the Jewish law again. In Chapter 5 Paul will warn the Christians in Galatia to resist such sneaky tactics and hang on to their new freedom tenaciously.

§ § § § § § §

The Message of Galatians 1:10–2:6

§ Paul is a servant of God who struggles with the dilemma of pleasing God or preaching a message that will be well received. He opts for the former task.

§ Paul sees himself in the tradition of Jesus, the humble servant.

§ § § § § § §

Galatians 2:7-21

Introduction to These Verses

In this section of Paul's letter to the Galatians, the Jerusalem Conference is still underway (see 2:1). Here Paul is concerned with ministry to various groups of people, a disagreement with Peter over the relationship between Jews and Gentiles, and the distinction between law and gospel. In the concluding verses of this section Paul reveals much about his own faith in Jesus Christ.

Establishment of Two Ministries (2:7-10)

The problem that Paul faced in Galatia was not really two different approaches to Christian ministry, but three. The first type of ministry was that characterized by the work of Peter, the mission to the circumcised (2:8). The second was that of Paul, the gospel to the uncircumcised (2:7). The third was that of Paul's opponents, the ones who sneaked in the false brethren in verse 4. The first ministry was conducted among Jewish people, and when they were converted to Christianity they were allowed, or perhaps required, to observe Jewish practices. Paul's ministry to the Gentiles was different, however. Since the Gentiles had never observed such practices, they were not asked to do so when they became Christians. The third group believed that the Gentiles also had to observe all of the Jewish rites to be Christian believers.

The conference that met in Jerusalem eliminated the influence of the third group altogether in the practice of mission. After the leaders of the Jerusalem church heard the outline of Paul's gospel (2:2), they realized that his preaching was the same as theirs, and they all agreed that there was only one gospel after all.

Paul says in 2:7-10 that it was decided that he and Barnabas should go to the Gentiles and that Jerusalem should minister to the circumcised. In Acts 15 Luke includes some of the dialogue that probably took place. Although Paul implies in Galatians that Peter went exclusively to the Jewish people to preach, it is more likely that his ministry was of a more mixed nature. According to Acts 10, Peter had also received revelation from God about a ministry he should perform among the Gentiles, and he was later to be remembered as the apostle most clearly identified with the city of Rome.

John (2:9) is the apostle John, who was one of Jesus' disciples. Although he is not mentioned in Acts 15 we know that, along with Peter and James the son of Zebedee, John was a leading figure among the first disciples and is often linked with Peter. (See Mark 1:29; 5:37; 9:2; 10:35-45; 14:33 and the parallel passages in Matthew and Luke; Acts 3–4.)

Verse 10 says that the *pillars* gave Barnabas and Paul the *right hand of fellowship*. The handshake represents the conclusion of an agreement between equals. Fellowship (*koinonia* in Greek) is the common bond shared by people who believe in Jesus Christ (1 Corinthians 1:9). The Lord's Supper is a fellowship (the Revised Standard Version reads *participation*) in the body of Christ (1 Corinthians 10:16). Fellowship is something that believers experience through the power of the Holy Spirit (2 Corinthians 13:14).

According to verse 10, the only piece of advice the Christian leaders in Jerusalem gave to Paul and Barnabas at the end of the Jerusalem conference was that they would have them remember the poor, to which Paul adds, *which very thing I was eager to do*. (Note that three very different suggestions are provided in Acts 15:19-20.) Helping the poor was an imperative that Christians inherited from the teachings of the Old Testament, and thus Paul could honestly say that he was eager to do so. The Jewish law had special provisions in it to make sure that those who were economically at the bottom of the ladder would be protected. Attention was to be paid to slaves, strangers, widows, orphans, and the poor as part of God's command (Exodus 22:21-27; 23:10-11). God is the God of the poor. God will hear their cries and help them (see Genesis 15:12-14; Deuteronomy 15:11-18; Psalms 3–6; 72:12-14).

In the New Testament the concern for the poor is also emphasized by Jesus and those who follow him. In his inaugural sermon Jesus says that he has come to preach good news to the poor and set the oppressed at liberty (Luke 4:16-30). His disciples are ordered to leave behind all material goods (Mark 6:6-11). They must not be attached to property if they want to avoid being separated from God (Mark 1:16-21; 10:17-30; Luke 9:59-62; 16:19-31).

The first believers took Jesus' teaching literally as they gave away their lands and goods to help the poor. The Jerusalem Christians shared everything they had (Acts 4:32) and distributed their goods to anyone in need (Acts 2:44-45). Apparently their conviction produced results at first, because they practically eliminated poverty in their midst. Eventually, the famines that developed during the time of the Roman Emperor Claudius (A.D. 41-57, see Acts 11:28-30) and general economic stress caused the Jerusalem church itself to go bankrupt, and it had to be helped with collections from other churches. Paul gave himself to the project with great devotion and energy (Romans 15:22-28). Acts 21:10-16 and 24:16-21 indicate that it was his eagerness to collect money for the impoverished church in Jerusalem that eventually led to his arrest and martyrdom in Rome.

Although Paul says nothing more in Galatians about how the churches of Galatia should help the poor, it is obvious that they did. In 1 Corinthians 16:1-4 he uses their generosity as an example to the Corinthian Christians.

Paul's Run-in With Peter (2:11-21)

The question: Should Jews and Gentiles have table fellowship? The word *but* in 2:11 indicates that the unity achieved over a handshake in Jerusalem was not always carried out later when it was tested in real circumstances. Christians can often agree to high standards in principle but waver from them in practice. Too often the power of faith is limited by the "buts" in life that cause us to turn aside from the very things we profess to believe the most. In the case Paul discusses in 2:11-21, Peter and James both violated the Jerusalem agreement. Paul says that Peter broke it by being wishy-washy in the faith: He ate first with the Gentiles; but then, seeing the men from James at another table, he changed seats. His motivation, in Paul's view, was fear. He was afraid that he would be criticized by the circumcision party for eating anything but kosher food.

The problem, of course, was not just one of food. It was one concerning the fellowship established in 2:9. Paul knew that the church could not be one if believers could not even sit down at the same table together. What is more, if they could not eat a meal together, how could they share the Lord's Supper, the clearest symbol of unity in Christ? Paul struggles with a similar issue in 1 Corinthians 11:17-33. There he is concerned that there was a rupture in table fellowship where the rich Christians came to the meeting early and had a sumptuous meal, while the poorer members ate alone later. By breaking table fellowship, by distinguishing between the rich and the poor in such a way, the Corinthians profaned the body of Christ (11:27). It is possible that Paul was worried about such a disregard for the poor in Galatians 2:11-21 as well (see 2:10).

Antioch (2:11) is a city on the Orontes River in northwestern Syria. Acts says that it was the first place where people were called Christians (Acts 11:26). It was an important meeting place for the early church (Acts 11:19-26; 14:26-28).

It is not clear who the certain *men who came from James* were. Whether or not James, the brother of Jesus, actually approved of their actions is not known. Probably he did if Paul includes him by name. (See the discussion of 1:19 for the background of James.) Possibly they were the same false brethren mentioned in 2:4 who wanted to impose Jewish standards on the Gentile converts. The fact that they were from James caused Peter to change tables. No doubt he felt safer politically by being with the more powerful men who were from Jerusalem. Peter's action influenced all the other Jews (2:13), and even Barnabas, Paul's traveling companion, insulted the Gentiles by moving. Paul's language about these activities is very descriptive.

Drew back (verse 12) is a military and political term which defines a retreat to a safer position. He puts it in the Greek imperfect tense to indicate that this was not an isolated incident but something which Peter customarily did. Paul's words literally mean *he kept on drawing back*. It reminds us of the word *deserting* in 1:6.

Separated in 2:12 is the same word Paul uses to describe his own selection as an apostle in 2:15 (*set me apart*). In Chapter 2 it indicates that Peter acted more like a Pharisee than a Christian by separating himself from his brothers and sisters in Christ (see the discussion of 2:15).

Insincerity in verse 13 is the English translation of the Greek *hypocrisis*, from which we get our word *hypocrisy*. In its most basic sense it means *pretense, play-acting*. Peter and the others were acting, they were insincere, when they first sat down with the Gentiles. Jesus repeatedly applies the same word to the hypocrisy of the Pharisees (Matthew 23:28; Mark 12:15; Luke 12:1; also see Matthew

23:13-15, 23-29; Mark 7:6; Luke 6:42).

Paul knows that Peter and the men from James are wrong in their actions in Antioch because such behavior denies the essential oneness of all Christians in Christ. Christians are united because Christ is one and because they are all saved from sin in the same way. Christ did not die on the cross so that the Jews could be saved by one method and the Gentiles by another. All people, whether Jews or Gentiles, are put right only by God's free gift in Christ; they are only justified by faith. In 2:14-21 Paul introduces his important concept of justification by faith alone, one which he expands in Galatians 3–4 and develops most fully in Romans 1:18–4:25. As he says in Romans 3:23-24, *all have sinned and fall short of the glory of God, they are justified by his grace.*

Throughout Galatians 2:14-21 and in the rest of the letter, the words *justify* and *justification* are very important. In its most basic sense justification refers to the taking away of guilt and making a person innocent. In English it is often translated *being put right* with God. Justification has a legal sense about it, indicating that someone must do something to remove guilt and create a not-guilty verdict. Paul argues in Romans that the normal sentence for human sin is the death penalty (Romans 6:23; see Genesis 3:19). The Jews believed that by observing the rules of the law (Galatians 2:16, 19; see the discussion in reference to 1:14) they could earn salvation. Paul denies that such a thing is possible. Being put right with God is only possible through faith in Jesus Christ (2:16). People cannot do anything to be put right with God, but they can believe in the power of God's action in Christ, that is, the raising of Jesus from the dead. They can believe that he is the Son of God (Romans 10:9). Then, and only then, will they be justified. Faith (2:16) means trust in God, who is himself trustworthy in every way. Paul says that we cannot get salvation the old-fashioned way—we cannot earn it.

Turning from Paul's concept of justification to the structure of Galatians 2:11-21 as a whole, it must be admitted that it is difficult to know just how the verses have been organized by him. Bible scholars are not certain where Paul's reprimand of Peter ends and his comments to the Galatians begin again. Probably the Revised Standard Version is correct when it puts quotation marks around the words in verse 14. In verse 15 Paul switches to *we*, which indicates that he is speaking to the Galatians again. In verses 18-21 he uses *I* and provides a personal example of what he means.

In verse 17 Paul poses a rhetorical question. Possibly some of the men from James may have put it to him to discredit his arguments. The question is: If we are put right with God through faith and are still found to be sinning anyway, do we not then make Christ an agent or a servant of sin? In other words, by falling back into sin, are we not making Christ's death on the cross useless, and actually forcing him to encourage sin? Paul's answer is a forceful *certainly not!* In Greek *certainly not* is a favorite expression of Paul's. Literally, it can be translated *God forbid, be it not so, by no means, nothing doing,* or *no way*. He uses it frequently in his writings to refute arguments against the truth of his gospel (Romans 3:3-6, 31; 6:2, 15; 7:7, 13; 9:14; 11:1, 11; 1 Corinthians 6:15; Galatians 3:21). The fact that Christians are still sinners does not nullify (Galatians 2:21) the grace of God. Justification is not determined by observance of the law, what the believer does not or does do. It is determined by what Christ did and what the believer believes.

In Galatians 2:19-20 Paul turns to some personal expressions of the meaning of faith that will help his readers understand their own relationship to Christ. These verses contain some of the most lyrical and beautiful words that Paul ever wrote and they, along with 1 Corinthians 13, have inspired Christians for centuries with their depth of feeling. Key expressions in these verses are *with Christ* and *in Christ*. Paul says that he is crucified with Christ; Christ lives in him; he lives by faith in the Son of God. These propositions of faith indicate how close Paul was to Jesus and why he knew that his gospel was true. Paul implies that the believer should be so close to Christ that Christ is part of the atmosphere that is breathed and inhaled. To use a modern example, it could be said that being in Christ is like a cup of hot tea. Christ is infused into the Christian like a teabag placed in a cup of hot water. Whether the teabag is in the water or the water is in the teabag is impossible to tell. Eventually the tea and the water are all the same as the tea flows into the water and the water goes through the teabag. Thus Paul can say that Christ is in him or that he is in Christ; it does not really matter. The image shows how much he feels the love of Christ in him and how much it influences every thought and action. For other places where Paul builds on the idea of being *in Christ* see Romans 3:24; 6:11, 23; 1 Corinthians 1:4; 2 Corinthians 2:17.

For Paul's use of the expression *crucified with Christ* see Romans 6:1-11 where he uses similar imagery. There he says that the Christian *dies to sin* through baptism, is *buried with Christ*, and then is *raised with him in newness of life*. The idea of taking part in Christ's sacrificial death is a favorite one of Paul's (Romans 8:17; Philippians 3:10; see Colossians 2:12-14; 3:1-4). The cross of Christ becomes the chief metaphor for the way the believer is delivered from the power of sin. It is a delivery from death to real life and freedom.

When Paul says in Galatians 2:19, *I through the law died to the law, that I might live to God,* he means that law is removed as a powerful force in his life, that it no longer has any control over him or claim upon him. To *live to God* is Paul's expression for true living, the very essence of life and the way a Christian acts on a day-to-day basis

(Galatians 5:25; Romans 6:8). Indeed, in a famous passage in Philippians 1:21, Paul shows that the meaning of life for him is entirely wrapped up in Jesus Christ when he says, *For me to live is Christ.*

§ § § § § § §

The Message of Galatians 2:7-21

§ Paul is entrusted with the gospel, to interpret it as best he can and to preach it to his audience.

§ Genuine disagreements and differences in interpretation of law and tradition characterized the early church just as they characterize today's church.

§ Faith in Jesus Christ is essential if one is to be justified (in right relationship with God).

§ § § § § § §

Galatians 3:1-21

Introduction to This Chapter

The significance of the words *justify* and *justification* has already been mentioned in reference to 2:14-21 in Part Four above. For Paul, justification by faith alone was the very heart of the gospel of Jesus Christ. Having been trained as a Pharisee, the revelation that he no longer needed to keep the law fully to be put right with God struck Paul like a lightning bolt. This knowledge was a miracle to him. Indeed, as he says in Romans 1:16, it was the very *power of God for salvation.*

Throughout the centuries Christians have often been moved by this same discovery. Martin Luther realized that the whole Roman Catholic system of making people think that they could earn their way into heaven was false, that they could be rescued from the power of sin only by faith in Christ. His commentary on Galatians is still exciting reading for those who want to share his discovery. Much later, in 1919, Karl Barth started a second reformation by his study of Paul's concept of justification in Romans. Barth's commentary on Romans opened the door to the neo-orthodox movement in Christian thinking, which still influences the church today.

Paul's understanding of the power of faith in Christ is still significant wherever people believe that you have to earn everything you get and that all should get exactly what they deserve. Throughout the rest of Galatians Paul shows that for Christians, what they get is dependent on what God gives in Christ, and what God gives is motivated by divine promises and love for the chosen people (3:8, 14, 18).

In this part of Galatians Paul shifts his style somewhat and generally abandons personal examples. Now he uses illustrations from the Old Testament and the experiences of the Galatians. In many ways Chapters 3 and 4 (along with Romans 3 and 4) are some of the most difficult parts of Paul's letters to understand. He believes that if he can prove a point from the Old Testament Scriptures his readers will be convinced that what he argues is absolutely true. His logic often escapes modern readers, however, and his proofs are not as convincing in the modern world as they were in the world in which he lived.

Have You Really Understood the Gospel? (3:1-5)

Paul returns in 3:1-5 to the pastoral concern which caused him to write his letter in the first place (1:6). He is worried because people in his churches are being led astray by a false teaching. He expresses his deep concern when he calls the Galatians *foolish* in verses 1 and 3. Probably he does not mean to be harsh here, but because he is a good pastor, he wants to get the attention of his members and save them from a serious spiritual mistake. The use of *foolish* and similar words is not unusual in "apologetic" letters (see the Introduction; also see Luke 24:25; Romans 1:14; Titus 3:3), and Paul's language indicates that the Galatians are slipping in their faith and are not using the spiritual powers of discernment which God has given them.

Bewitched probably refers to the belief in the ancient world that enemies could give you an "evil eye". Possibly the Galatians have drifted so far from what Paul originally taught them that he is wondering if someone has cast a spell on them. In 5:20 he warns them that sorcery is one of the things which could keep them out of God's kingdom.

Before whose eyes Jesus Christ was publicly portrayed as crucified refers to the teaching about Christ that Paul and others have delivered to the Galatians. One of the goals of an ancient orator was to make his message so vivid that his readers could form a mental picture in their own imaginations. Sometimes he would even use acting gestures or paintings to make his point. Paul has preached about the crucifixion and resurrection of Jesus so often that the Galatians should be able to see these events like a videotape, playing and replaying in their minds. But someone has bewitched them and kept them from visualizing the truth anymore. Paul's understanding of the importance of Christ's crucifixion will be discussed in more detail in relation to 3:10-14.

In verses 2-5 Paul asks a set of important questions. Did the Galatians receive the Spirit through the law or through the hearing of faith? The answer is obvious. They became Christians by hearing Paul's preaching and seeing Christ publicly portrayed. Why, then, are they turning back to the law for spiritual benefits?

Paul mentions the Holy Spirit for the first time in Galatians in verses 2-5 (see 3:14; 4:6, 29; 5:5, 16, 18, 22, 25; 6:8). In these verses he refers to the Galatians' own spiritual experiences. They should know from their own lives that it is the Spirit who makes alive and not the letter of the law. *Having begun in the Spirit* seems to indicate that many of the Galatians had charismatic experiences when they accepted Jesus as Lord (see Acts 2). God works miracles among them through the Spirit. The Spirit helps them understand the Old Testament. It enables them to pray. Paul discusses sanctification and the fruits of the Spirit in 5:22-24, and in 5:25 concludes that people who have the Spirit in them should walk accordingly.

The Greek word for Spirit is *pneuma*. It means both *wind* and *spirit*. The Holy Spirit is like a fresh, powerful wind blowing through the lives of the Galatians (see John

3:6-8) which cleanses them and gives them new life. In 6:1 he compliments them by calling them *pneumatics (you who are spiritual)*. Those who know what the gifts of the Spirit are (see 1 Corinthians 12:1-11) should not so easily be deflected back to dependence on an inert law which brings death instead of life.

In verse 3 Paul uses another set of opposites to help the Galatians understand belief in Jesus Christ. In other places he uses the contrasting images of faith versus law, life versus death. Here he uses Spirit versus flesh. Although he will define flesh more completely in 5:16-21, it needs to be noted here that when Paul opposes it to Spirit he usually means the attitude and habits in human nature that are opposed to God. He especially means those that depend on the law or circumcision for justification (4:23,29; 5:13; 6:8, 12, 13; also see Romans 6:19; 7:5). In a particularly moving passage in Romans, Paul makes it clear that human nature and the desires of the flesh will let him down time after time (Romans 7:18-24). He asks himself there who will deliver him from his body of death. The answer is found in Romans 8:2 and is the same one implied in Galatians 3: God did what the law could not do. God sent Jesus Christ in the likeness of sinful flesh and condemned sin.

The Example of Abraham (3:6-9)

Paul sets out in the rest of Chapter 3 to prove his case to the Galatians from Old Testament Scriptures. He quotes them six times in the next few verses: 3:6—Genesis 15:6; 3:8—Genesis 12:3; 3:10—Deuternomony 27:26; 3:11—Habakkuk 2:4; 3:12—Leviticus 18:5; 3:13—Deuteronomy 21:23.

Galatians 3 and 4 are very similar to Romans 3:21-4:25, and the four chapters need to be compared to understand Paul's thinking completely.

In 3:6 Paul introduces the example of Abraham for the first time, and it serves as a major illustration throughout the rest of Chapters 3–4. Why does Paul choose Abraham? Because Abraham was the parent of the Jewish religion. Paul knows that if he can prove his case about the Christian faith by referring to him, his readers will be convinced that the gospel has been in God's plan from the beginning. Since Abraham became a believer in God before the Ten Commandments (the law) came, and since he even believed before circumcision came, Paul hopes to prove what God really intends by going back to the beginning of faith, that is, back to Abraham. Throughout Jewish tradition Abraham was a very important figure, as references in the New Testament show (Matthew 1:1, 2, 17; 3:9; Luke 16:22-30; John 8:58; Acts 7:2-17; Hebrews 7:1-10; 11:8; 1 Peter 3:6).

Abraham provides a particularly important illustration of what faith means, what trust in God means, because Abraham believed without doing anything or being able to see proof of God's promise. The story begins in Genesis 12 where God promises to make Abram (his name is changed to Abraham in Genesis 17:5) the father of a multitude of nations (see Galatians 3:8). Since Abram is very old he cannot see how he could be the father of one child, much less millions of children. But God promises and then delivers Isaac to Abraham and Sarah in their old age (Genesis 17; 21). Isaac's birth and circumcision become signs of God's contract or covenant with Israel (Genesis 17:9-14). Paul's argument in Galatians is that since Abraham believed in God and obeyed him before circumcision ever existed, circumcision is an incidental and not an essential of faith. In verse 8 he contends that the real children of God are Gentiles, because they did not believe in the law or circumcision, but only believed God's promises in Jesus Christ. Paul presents the same argument in more detail in Romans 9:6-33. This was all God's plan from the beginning. So much so, Paul says, that Abraham actually had the gospel, the good news of Christ, previewed to him (*preached the gospel beforehand to Abraham,* verse 8).

The word *blessed* in verses 8 and 9 refers to the important concept of cursing and blessing in the Scriptures. The basic idea is that human beings live under God's curse if they are disobedient, but are under God's blessing and promise if they have faith and are obedient. God's blessing is placed on humanity from the very beginning (Genesis 1:28), but the curse comes with the introduction of sin into the world (Genesis 3:16-19; 4:8-16). Although the curse continues throughout Genesis 11, God begins a new covenant with Abraham (12:1-3). Paul sees this change as the most powerful Old Testament example of the new covenant in Christ, and he will continue to explore it in Galatians 3:10-14 and 15-18.

Rescue From the Curse of the Law (3:10-14)

In these verses Paul quotes Old Testament Scriptures four times to prove his case (3:10—Deuteronomy 27:26; 3:11—Habakkuk 2:4; 3:12—Leviticus 18:5; 3:13—Deuteronomy 21:23).

In verse 10 he picks up the idea of the curse of God, the very opposite of the blessing mentioned in verse 9. Quoting Deuteronomy 27:26, Paul argues that anyone who tries to keep the law must keep all aspects of it to avoid being condemned. Since it is impossible for any human being to do this because of the power of sin (see Romans 7:13-25; 11:32), those who try to keep the law are under the curse mentioned in the discussion above (3:9).

For it is written is an expression Paul uses as a formula to introduce a quotation of Scripture (see Galatians 4:22; Romans 12:19; 1 Corinthians 1:19).

In verse 11 he reinforces his argument by quoting Habakkuk 2:4, *He who through faith is righteous shall live.* By citing this text he provides another example which shows that the idea of being put right with God by faith alone is nothing new, but was already in the Old Testament. (See Romans 3:21-22.) He quotes the same words from Habakkuk in a famous verse in Romans 1:17.

In verse 12 Paul quotes Leviticus 18:5 to show that the law cannot rest on faith since *he who does them shall live by them*. Paul implies here once again that it is not the doing of the law (which is really impossible), but the believing of faith, that results in God's promise. A close examination of the passage in Leviticus shows that Paul has really not proved his case by quoting it here. In Leviticus 18:5 the point that Moses makes is that those who keep all of the statutes of the law will live. Paul twists it around to mean just the opposite, namely that those who (try to) keep the law will surely die.

Paul goes on to demonstrate in verse 13 that the curse that automatically falls on those who will not or cannot keep the law is not canceled because one becomes a Christian. In Paul's view the law has to be fulfilled. But how is that possible? How can one be given a death penalty and still live in the Spirit? It is fulfilled, Paul argues, by the action of Christ. Christ redeems believers from the inevitable curse of the law by taking that curse upon himself.

Paul cites Deuteronomy 21:23 in verse 13 to prove that by hanging on a tree (*tree* is often a synonym for cross), Jesus completed the requirement of the law. The original idea in Deuteronomy was that anyone who was sentenced to death should be hung on a gallows or wooden stake. It was forbidden, however, to leave the body there overnight, since the one hanged was cursed by God and would pollute the whole land. Usually the criminal was hung on a timber, probably by the hands, in public (see Galatians 3:1, *publicly portrayed*), until dead. In Paul's view, Jesus, by dying on the cross, suffered the public humiliation required by the law for sin.

Here it is possible to see how Paul and other Christians after him were able to understand a terrible instrument of death as a symbol of hope and life. The cross, which was a painful means of punishing criminals through a slow, agonizing death in which the victim died from asphyxiation and exposure, now becomes the symbol of God's forgiveness and love. For Paul the cross is one of the chief symbols of the love of God (Galatians 2:20; 6:12; Romans 6:6; 1 Corinthians 1:13; 2 Corinthians 13:4).

Redeemed in verse 13 refers in its most basic sense to the exchange of an object or a person for some kind of payment. In Leviticus 25:25-34, for example, it is said that if a man becomes poor and sells his property to pay his debts, it is up to his brother to buy it back and redeem it. In 25:47-50 the same thing is to happen if he sells himself as a slave: He is to be redeemed by his brother. Later the term is applied to God as the one who does the redeeming (Job 19:25; Psalm 19:14; 78:35; Proverbs 23:11; Isaiah 41:14; 43:14; 54:5; 60:16).

In Paul's writings and the rest of the New Testament this important idea is applied to Jesus: Through Jesus God has "bought back" the people from the curse of the law, from the slavery it imposes. Through his love Christ has made them free (Mark 10:45; 14:24; Romans 3:24; 8:23; 1 Corinthians 1:30; 6:20; Galatians 4:5). Paul makes sure in Galatians 3:14 that the promise of the redemption is personalized: Christ brought the blessing of Abraham to the Gentiles, *that we might receive the promise of the Spirit.*

God Gives a Covenant and a Promise (3:15-21)

Paul switches ground in these verses and now provides a *human example*. By that he means that he will give an illustration from everyday life instead of from Scripture. The example is from the court procedures of the ancient world. It is not possible, Paul argues, to have a will changed once it has been made. There would be no point in making it at all if the desires of the person making it could easily be set aside. The Greek word which Paul uses for *will* is the same word he uses for *covenant* in verse 17. For Paul, a will and a covenant are similar. A will is a contract a person makes in the courts in which certain things are promised. A covenant is a contract a king makes with another king or another nation in which certain things are also promised. Just as a person makes out a will to pass on property to heirs, so God made a covenant with Israel to pass on redemption to the chosen people. The covenant that God made was to Abraham and his offspring (verse 16). Since, as Paul has argued already in verses 6-14, the contract was made with Abraham on the basis of faith and a promise, it could not be arbitrarily changed 430 years later (verse 17), to depend on circumcision and the law. To do so would be to make God break the contract with the chosen people.

In verse 16 Paul makes a play on words to prove his point. Unfortunately it is not one which is necessarily very convincing to modern readers. It sounds, in a way, like a bad sermon illustration that makes everyone wonder why it was given in the first place. In verse 16, Paul points out that in the Greek version of Genesis 17:7-8 the word *offsprings* (*descendants* in the Revised Standard Version) is not plural but singular, *offspring*. This he knows from the Greek, which is *sperma* (seed, sperm, child). In Paul's view, this singular noun proves that God originally intended redemption to come through Abraham, not through all of his many descendants. It is to come only through his one true descendant, Jesus Christ. If Christ is the one to whom the true promise is given, then it is also to the Galatians and other Christians who share Christ's inheritance as adopted children (see Galatians 4:5, 7). Whether or not the original writer of Genesis wished to emphasize the singular *offspring* is hard to say. If so, it would have been only in relation to Isaac, the true son of Abraham, not Christ. But even if Paul had understood the Genesis text that way he would have made the same point anyway, because in his view, Isaac stands as a symbol for the truth which later was to be revealed in Christ (Galatians 4:21-31).

Four hundred and thirty years (verse 17) is apparently

GALATIANS AND EPHESIANS

derived from Exodus 12:40, the Old Testament calculation of the time between the giving of the promise to Abraham and the giving of the law to Moses. The long period involved allows Paul to show how unjust it would be to break the agreement made with Abraham, since it was made so many years before the law came.

Inheritance (verse 18; see 4:1, 7, 30; 5:21) refers to all of the benefits believers can claim by becoming children of God. In 1 Corinthians 6:9-10 Paul lists all of the people who will not inherit the Kingdom (see Galatians 5:21; Ephesians 5:5). Paul's main idea in Galatians is that inheritance is not something one receives automatically as a right from God, as if it could be earned by simply being born or by doing right things. Instead, inheritance comes through adoption (Galatians 4:5) by God. Since no one deserves God's blessings and they only come by faith, all inheritance comes through God's gift of adoption (see Romans 4:13-14; 8:17; Ephesians 1:14, 18). If the law cannot earn God's favor, then what good is it? Paul asks in verses 19 and 20. It was added because of transgressions, that is, it was produced by God as a temporary measure so that sin could be held in check until the promise would come. Paul develops the idea of the law as a check and balance with more clarity in 3:23-27, where he defines it as a *tutor*. The offspring who had to come before the law was relieved of its duties was, of course, Jesus Christ (3:16).

Ordained by angels probably refers to the belief in Jewish tradition that the law or Torah was given to the Jews by angels. The *intermediary* in verses 19-20 is Moses. Although it is not clear exactly what Paul means here, he no doubt has in mind the idea that although God gave the covenant and promise directly to Abraham, the law came from angels and Moses, and this proves the law's inferiority.

Is the law against the promise, then? Paul asks in verse 21. The answer, *certainly not*, is the same one given in

2:17 (see the discussion there). The law has a positive, restraining function because it consigns all things to sin. In Galatians this means that the law was designed to keep people from sin as much as possible until they could be released from it through Christ. In Romans Paul goes a step further and argues that the law actually encourages sin (4:14; 5:20-21; 7:4-13), so that the grace of God may be revealed more clearly.

§ § § § § § §

The Message of Galatians 3

§ Justification by faith is the heart of the Christian gospel, according to Paul.

§ Justification by faith is more important than the Old Testament conception of law.

§ The law did have a reason for existence, however. The law existed so that sin would be evident to human beings.

§ § § § § § §

Galatians 3:22–4:31

Introduction to These Verses

In Chapter 4 of Galatians, Paul discusses more fully his idea of the law and how it relates to the gospel. Whereas in Chapter 3 the discussion focused on the Old Testament concept of law, in this chapter Paul's thoughts center on what that law means when viewed from the perspective of the coming of Christ. Paul also speaks of his dissatisfaction over the spiritual attitude of the Galatians.

The Law as Tutor and Other Examples (3:22–4:7)

Galatians 3:22–4:7 defines more clearly what Paul considers the positive value of the law by his use of the word *tutor* (*custodian* in the Revised Standard Version). The Greek word that he uses here has been rendered in many different ways in different translations: *schoolmaster, one in charge of us, one who held us as wards in discipline,* even *babysitter.* What Paul refers to in verse 24, when he says that the law was our custodian until Christ came, is the practice in the ancient world of hiring a disciplinarian, often an educated slave, to take care of children while they were in school. The pedagogue was not a teacher but was the one who took the children back and forth to school and made sure that they did their work. His job was to protect the students from attack outside of the home and teach them good manners. Tutors often had a reputation for being tough and had the authority to beat unruly boys. The boys were usually under their rule until they reached maturity.

Paul sees the law as playing the same necessary role. The law was needed to bring humanity to maturity in Jesus Christ. Although it had a role which was largely negative because it told people what they should not do, it also contained in its essence the very basic principles of God's kingdom. Indeed, the Ten Commandments can easily be divided into the two basic laws which Paul saw as a summary of God's law, "love God" (Exodus 20:1-11) and "love your neighbor as yourself" (Exodus 20:12-17; Galatians 5:14). Nevertheless, for Paul, the role played by the law is limited. It ends when the Christian reaches faith in Christ, and maturity (verse 25). It ends now that faith has come, that is, when Christ has come and justification by faith is made possible through him and his coming into the history of the world.

A similar idea is used to describe the law's function in 4:1-3 when Paul continues the metaphor of the believer as the adopted child of God (see the discussion of inheritance in 3:18 above). In the ancient world, if a child's father died while he was still under age, he was placed under the control of a guardian or trustees (4:2). Like the will mentioned in 3:15, this legal contract placed the boy under the guardian's care until he reached legal age. Until that time, the child had to obey as if he were the guardian's slave, even though, in fact, he was the master of the house. The believer, under the law, was like that child, under the control of the law's guardianship. But under Christ the Christian is no longer a spiritual minor and does not remain under the trusteeship of the law. He or she has become a child in every sense and an heir through faith in Christ (4:7). This happened at a particular point in history, when faith came (3:25), when Jesus Christ was born at a certain time, at a certain place, to certain parents, when the time had fully come, when God sent forth a Son, born of woman, born under the law, to redeem those who were under the law, so that we might receive adoption as children of God.

When the time had fully come implies that all of history was struggling under the tutelage of the law, writhing under the evil influence of sin. But *when the fullness of time came,* as the Greek may be literally translated, when just the right time arrived according to God's eternal plan, then Christ came, and the law was ushered out and grace and the promise were brought in (see Mark 1:15; Ephesians 1:10; Hebrews 1:2).

In 4:3-7 Paul interweaves a second metaphor with that of the minor inheriting an estate. In verse 3 he introduces the illustration of the slave under the control of *the elemental spirits of the universe.* Paul's belief that Christians are liberated from all kinds of spiritual and social slavery runs all through Galatians (see the discussions of 3:27-29; 5:1).

Elemental spirits of the universe refers to demonic forces which people of the ancient world believed were in control of the universe. For a close parallel see Colossians 2:8, 20; 2 Peter 3:10-12. These elements dominated the present evil age (1:4). The universe, according to this belief system, was controlled by the essential forces of earth, air, fire, and water, and they had personalities. They were living spiritual beings. Gentiles and Jews alike often considered themselves to be totally under the power of these spirits so that everything they did was subjected to them. Jews sometimes worshiped these spirits by combining their worship with the observance of Jewish special days, special months, seasons, or years (4:10; see Colossians 2:15-18).

Paul worries that the Galatians may still be influenced by these spirits, and thus he tells them in verse 8 that they are not real beings at all, they are beings that by nature are not gods. They are weak and beggarly elemental spirits (4:9), because they really do not exist. The Galatians, before they became Christians, before they believed in God (4:8), were enslaved to such false ideas.

Now that they are liberated in Christ they must not fall back under their control.

In 4:4 the expression *born of woman* means that Jesus came in human history, through normal human parents, to liberate those who believe in him. It stresses his humanity and the fact that, like any human being, he was influenced by the culture in which he found himself (*born under the law*). Paul never mentions the virgin birth of Jesus, and he does not have it in mind here.

In 4:6 Paul points out the great difference between the fear produced by belief in the elemental spirits and the closeness to God created by the Holy Spirit. *God has sent the Spirit of the Son into our hearts, crying, "Abba, Father!"* *Abba* is an Aramaic word that means *my father* or *our father*. Paul and other Greek-speaking Christians probably used it in prayers and services of worship because it was one of Jesus' favorite words. According to Mark 14:36, Jesus used it in his most desperate hour, in the Garden of Gethsemane. *Abba* is a very intimate form of address and literally means *Daddy* or *Dad*. It implies no disrespect, but shows that Jesus taught his disciples that, as Paul says in Galatians 3:29 and 4:3-6, his followers truly are children of God and are as close to God as children normally are to their parents. There is no reason why the Christian cannot be close to God. Jesus teaches us to use the word *Father* and the Holy Spirit cries it out for us. Possibly Paul's readers thought of the first line of the Lord's Prayer when they heard the word *Abba*, remembering how Jesus taught them that they could be like children and ask God for all things.

No Distinction in Christ! (3:27-29)

This important section was passed over in the discussion above in order to follow the flow of Paul's argument about the law. In 3:27-29 he digresses for a moment to speak about the practical effects of being children of God. Although this passage is very short, it provides a significant key to Paul's thinking about social relationships in the Christian church. He switches from *we* to *you* in verse 27 because he wants the Galatians to think about the way they should treat each other in their own faith community. The closest parallels are found in 1 Corinthians 12:13, where he discusses the body of Christ (the church), and Colossians 3:9-11, which is concerned about the new nature God gives believers in Christ (the new creation).

In Galatians 3 Paul implies that because all believers are children of God, and all Christians are one in Christ, all distinctions based on racial, political, religious, social, or sexual grounds must be dissolved. Jews and Greeks, because of faith in Christ, are all one in him. Slaves and slave owners are equal in him because they are all servants of Jesus Christ. Although Paul nowhere urges the church to fight against the evil institution of slavery (see Philemon; Colossians 3:22-25; and the discussion of Ephesians 6:5-9), he expects that slaves will be full members of the Christian church. What is more, he wants the distinctions between men and women to fall as well. Despite the fact that Paul's attitude is not consistently liberal toward women (see 1 Corinthians 7:39-40; 11:2-16), in Galatians he clearly implies that they have equal rights in the church and are equal in Christ. Paul often considered women full partners in ministry and depended on their spiritual and financial support (Acts 16:14-15; 18:1-4, 18; Romans 16:1-6, 12-13, 15; Colossians 4:15). On the basis of these verses and Galatians 3:28, it is fair to say that there is no room for discrimination against women in ministry in any church or denomination that claims to be Christ's.

Paul grounds Christian equality in the concept of baptism. *For as many of you as were baptized in Christ have put on Christ* (verse 27). He uses references to baptism in many different ways in his writings, so it is difficult to know exactly what he means here (see Romans 6:3-4; 1

Corinthians 1:13-17; 12:13; 15:29; Colossians 2:12). The closest passages appear to be Romans 6:3-4 and 1 Corinthians 12:13. In Galatians Paul implies that baptism, since it is a common Christian symbol, shows what it means for Christians to be "in Christ" and to have Christ "in" them (2:20). All Christians are one because they are incorporated in him, they have been washed clean by him, and they are part of his one body (1 Corinthians 12). As Ephesians 4:4-5 says, *there is one body and one Spirit, one Lord, one faith,* (and) *one baptism.*

Put on Christ is a dynamic image that Paul has borrowed from early Christian baptism services. Before that service, the new Christian took off his or her outer garment. This action symbolized putting off the old nature. After baptism, the person was given a new, white robe symbolizing the new nature in Christ and the cleansing of the Holy Spirit. For Paul, Christ was as close to him as his own clothing, and since he and other Christians had all "put on" Christ, they all looked alike to God and there were no longer any grounds for social discrimination in the church. Paul often uses the image of "putting on Christ" or "the new creation" to speak about the new order that Christ brings (1 Corinthians 15:53-54; 2 Corinthians 5:3-4; Colossians 3:10-14; also see Ephesians 4:22-24).

Do Not Go Back to Slavery! (4:8-20)

In this section Paul leaves the argument of the law for a moment and expresses some of his deep pastoral concerns. He is worried, first of all, that the Galatians may fall back under the influence of old superstititions about elemental spirits. (See the discussion of 4:3 above.) He is also worried in verse 10 that they may become trapped in meticulous observances of religious calendars or astrology in which the believer is always observing the day, month, season, year, moon, or planets to find out what to do and what not to do. Recent studies indicate that such observances were regularly practiced by Jews in the Dead Sea area and by Gentiles all over the Roman Empire.

Paul is also worried that the Galatians' attitude toward him may change (4:12-16). When he first visited them they were very kind to him and gave him every consideration. They even took care of him when he was sick (verse 13, *bodily ailment*). It is not possible to be sure what this illness was. It may have had to do with eye problems (see 6:11) brought on by his Damascus road experience. Or possibly it was a recurrence of "the thorn in the flesh" mentioned in 2 Corinthians 12:7. Whatever the illness was, the Galatians ministered to him, treating him as if he were an angel or Christ himself (compare Matthew 25:31-46).

You would have plucked out your eyes and given them to me in verse 15 indicates that at that time the Galatians would have done anything for him, they loved and respected him so much. Now, of course, things have changed radically and his enemies have turned them against him. He hopes that they will return to their former good feelings even though he is far away (verse 18).

In verses 19-20 he ends the section on a note of pastoral love and affection (*change my tone*, verse 20). *My little children* contrasts sharply with Paul's reprimands in 1:6, 3:1, and 4:9. Here he indicates that he is the Galatians' spiritual mother (*I am in travail until Christ be formed in you*). *Travail* refers to the labor pains a mother feels when a baby is being delivered (see Revelation 12:2). Even though Paul refers to himself as a nursemaid in 1 Thessalonians 2:7 and the father of other congregations in 1 Corinthians 4:15, 1 Thessalonians 2:11, and Philemon 10, his statement is still striking here. Perhaps he wants to stress his maternal duties to the Galatian churches because although he *gave birth* to them once (4:13; 1:8), he is worried that they will have to be reborn in Christ all over again if they continue to wander from the faith (see 6:16).

Allegory of the Two Children (4:21-31)

Paul returns to his argument about the law and faith with a question in 4:21. The section is an allegory based on the story of Abraham and Sarah and Abraham's two sons, Ishmael and Isaac, in Genesis 16–18 and 21. An allegory is a story in which nearly every major detail or character stands for something else.

According to the story in Genesis, after God had promised that all the nations of the earth would be blessed in Abraham (Genesis 12:3), Abraham was worried that he was too old to have children. Sarah, his wife, encouraged him to have a baby with Hagar, a concubine, so a son of promise could be born. Ishmael was then born. Later, however, when Abraham and Sarah miraculously had their own son, Sarah insisted that Hagar and her child be thrown out of the household.

Paul sees in this story another illustration of the superiority of faith over law. His understanding of the allegory is that since Hagar and Ishmael were thrown out of the house of faith, so the law must now be thrown out of the church and out of the individual Christian's life. Paul has already said that the Galatians are children of God in Christ and no longer slaves (4:1-7). So they must not think of themselves as children of the slave mother but offspring of the free woman of faith.

Paul's argument here may have been very convincing to Jewish Christians who were accustomed to thinking this way, but it often leaves modern readers cold. Even though its logic is clear enough, it not likely to lead Christians to spiritual freedom in today's world.

Arabia means the desert penisula between Egypt and Israel, not the Arabia in 1:17. The quotation in 4:27 is from Isaiah 54:1.

§ § § § § § §

The Message of Galatians 3:22–4:31

§ This section concentrates on defining Paul's concept of justification by faith alone through examples from the Old Testament Scriptures and the experiences of the Galatian Christians.

§ Paul shows that since Abraham, the father of the Jewish faith, received God's promise before circumcision and the Ten Commandments came into the world, faith is superior to the law. Even though the law requires that a punishment or curse be upon those who have not kept it, Christ has taken the curse upon himself to give the promise to those who believe in him.

§ An example from legal proceedings demonstrates the same point. Just as a will cannot be broken, so God will not break the contract (covenant) made with Abraham before the law was given.

§ The law served a function as a spiritual disciplinarian, but now that faith has come it is no longer needed. Now those who believe have full rights as children of God.

§ Paul hopes that the Galatians will remember their affection for him and trust in the gospel. He is worried about them and hopes that they will not need to be reborn in Christ.

§ § § § § § §

Galatians 5

Introduction to This Chapter

Here Paul begins a section in the final portion of his
letter which brings exhortation or moral advice to his
readers. Many of his letters end in a similar manner (2
Corinthians 13:5-11; Philippians 3:1-4:9; 1 Thessalonians
4:1–5:22).

For Freedom Christ Has Set Us Free (5:1)

For freedom Christ has set us free. Paul has already
mentioned that freedom is a special thing to have since
spiritual slavery is always a temptation and a distinct
possibility at any time in the Christian life (see 2:4; 4:1-7,
21-31). The Christian is given the gift of freedom by God
through Christ to be free from several things: the
elemental spirits (4:3, 9), fear (2:12), false teachers (3:1;
2:4; 1:9) and discrimination (3:28). In Chapter 5 he also
lists several specific evil habits and attitudes from which
the believer may also be liberated.

The key to Christian freedom, as Paul points out, is the
Holy Spirit (5:16). The Holy Spirit is the encouraging
force of God, the moving, powerful morale booster which
liberates and makes free. The Spirit "blows" the believer
to new levels of spiritual creativeness. Simply put, *Now
the Lord is the Spirit, and where the Spirit of the Lord is, there
is freedom* (2 Corinthians 3:17).

The freedom that Christ brings was especially important
to many of Paul's Galatian readers who were trying to
decide whether or not to adopt Jewish practices again. As

John 8:31-59 demonstrates, some Jews thought that they were already free without Christ because they were children of Abraham. Jesus points out, however, that they really are slaves to sin and do not understand the truth of God. Similarly in Galatians, Paul worries that the Galatians may try to become children of Abraham through circumcision and the law only to become the children of slavery again (4:21-31).

Stand fast in 5:1 is a military term and means that the Galatians have to fight for their freedom and actively preserve it. They must not yield to the onslaughts of sin.

Yoke of slavery is a familiar image in the New Testament (Matthew 11:29-30; Acts 15:10; 1 Timothy 6:1). Jesus says in Matthew 11 that his yoke of Christian duty is easy to carry and fits just right. The law, however, for Paul, is an intolerable burden and leads to restriction (Galatians 3:22, 23-25; 4:1-3) and death.

Through Love, Faith Liberates Us (5:2-6)

Paul repeats what has been already said: If you keep the law, you lose Christ. If you accept circumcision you have to keep the whole law (see Romans 2:17–3:21), and since it is impossible to do that all people who try it fall under the power of sin. (See the discussion of 3:10-14 above.)

You are severed from Christ in verse 4 means that for those who try to keep the law, Christ is made ineffective or powerless. His grace is abolished or wiped out for them. The same word *severed* is translated from Greek into English in Romans 3:3 as *nullify*, *overthrow* in Romans 3:31, *bring to nothing* in 1 Corinthians 1:28 and *destroy* in 1 Corinthians 6:13.

In verses 5 and 6 Paul focuses on the real meaning of freedom in Spirit. It leads to hope and love. Here, as in 1 Corinthians 13:13, faith, hope, and love are brought together (also in 1 Thessalonians 1:3; 5:8) and once again the greatest priority is given to love. Faith working through love, not through the law, is the operative key of faith.

The kind of love Paul means specifically is *agape* love, self-giving love, generous love, love that is unlimited and willing to sacrifice for the other person. Love is freedom, in essence, because it lets the self go and is directed only to God and to the other. Agape love is the kind of love that Jesus gave to humanity through his death and resurrection. By following his example Christians can really be free. Love is the first fruit of the Spirit (Galatians 5:22); it is the best gift of the Spirit (1 Corinthians 13:13). Love is the more excellent way. Agape love was such an important thing to the first Christians that it is mentioned more than one hundred times in the New Testament.

If agape love is something that the Christian may experience here and now, hope (verse 4) is something which will only be realized fully in the future. Hope is that quality that keeps the eye of faith focused upon God's plan for the future and believes without seeing it completely carried out. Hope looks to the end of time to see how all of God's promises will be kept. Thus in Romans 8:23-26, Paul says that hope is not what is seen but what is not seen. Those who have the first fruits of the Spirit (see Galatians 5:22) wait for adoption as God's children, for the redeeming of the body. *Faith is the assurance of things hoped for, the conviction of things not seen* (Hebrews 11:1). God is a God of hope (Romans 15:13), and God gave us the Scriptures to enable us to continue in it (Romans 15:4). For Paul, hope is particularly connected with freedom in the Spirit because whereas the law kills, the Spirit gives life (2 Corinthians 3:6). *Hope does not disappoint us, because God's love has been poured into our hearts through the Holy Spirit which has been given to us* (Romans 5:5). The Christian is no longer saved by performing works through the law, but by faith working through love. The hope of righteousness is that vision of the future which every Christian has that enables him or her to know with asssurance that God will forgive all sin and bring salvation at the last.

An Angry Aside (5:7-12)

In 5:7-12 Paul returns to his concern about the influence his opponents continue to have on the Galatian Christians. In terms similar to those in 1:6 and 3:1, Paul wonders what has caused those he has trained to lose the race of faith. They were running the race well and Paul would like to know who tripped them and put them in danger of not being able to finish. (See Paul's use of track and field images in the discussion of 2:2 above.) Once again he reminds them that the ideas that are disqualifying them are not things that he coached them to believe (verse 8).

Verse 9 uses a parable that was familiar in the ancient world. It means that just a small piece of yeast is enough to cause a whole loaf of bread to rise. Paul uses it in 1 Corinthians 5:6-8 to make the same point. Jesus employs it several times as well (Matthew 13:33; 16:6; Mark 8:15; Luke 12:1; 13:21). In Galatians it appears to mean that a little bit of bad influence goes a long way. "Ignore the bad teaching of the false brethren," Paul is saying, "and return to my gospel" (see verse 10).

Verse 11 is difficult to understand. *But if I still preach circumcision* probably points to criticisms Paul's opponents were using to discredit his preaching. Possibly they were accusing him of having preached circumcision while he was still a Pharisee, or of having been wishy-washy in deciding which Christians should be circumcised and which ones should not (contrast Galatians 2:3 with Acts 16:3). Paul shows that the accusations are obviously false. If he preached circumcision his enemies would not be persecuting him because then he would agree with them. What is more, if he preached circumcision, he would be removing the stumbling block of the cross and making it easier for them to accept. The stumbling block (*skandalon* in Greek) refers to an obstacle that can cause a person to trip and fall. In 1 Corinthians 1:23 Paul says that the cross is a stumbling block to the Jews, probably because they want salvation to come through the law, not through the forgiveness given by Christ's death and resurrection. (See Romans 9:32-33.) If Paul had preached circumcision, he would have removed his enemies' major objection. As it is, since he is true to the gospel, the offense of the cross remains, and he is still persecuted.

In verse 12 Paul concludes this section with a bawdy, coarse joke. It takes little imagination to visualize what he means. If my enemies are so determined to circumcise themselves, he implies, I hope that they slip and really cut themselves (mutilate themselves)! If they are castrated then they will get what they deserve. Instead of being children of God they can all be eunuchs (many pagan religions required priests to be eunuchs) in service of their false god, the law.

Love Calls Us to Serve One Another (5:13-15)

Paul reiterates what already has been said in 5:1: The Christian has been called for freedom. But care must be taken. Christian freedom can lead to license so that terrible things like those listed in 5:18-20 take place. *Opportunity for the flesh* is a military term that provides the picture of a soldier giving ground to the enemy, allowing him opportunity to win the battle. Since the Christian life is a battleground where good and evil struggle for control, the Christian cannot yield an inch by adopting unchristian habits or attitudes. The same idea is used in Romans 7:8 and 11. For the meaning of the word *flesh* see the discussion of 3:4 above.

How, then, does the Christian win the battle (verses 14-15)? Only through agape love (see the discussion of 5:6). The rules of the law are not necessary to be put right with God or to live the right life. If one follows the true intent of the law that is spelled out in Leviticus 19:18

and taught by Jesus (Matthew 22:39), there will be no defeats at the hand of evil. If all people would love neighbors as much as themselves there would never be a need for a battle in the first place. The self-giving love taught by the Old Testament and lived by Jesus removes the need for rules, traditions, and works of law (Romans 13:8), because it focuses on that which is at God's heart, the love that gives itself away. But, Paul warns, if you continue to live like wild animals and snap at each other and try to eat each other up, if you do not love and serve one another, you had better be careful or your hatred for each other will swallow all of you. Loving one another, as the New Testament constantly teaches, is a primary characteristic of being a Christian (Galatians 6:10; Romans 13:9-10; James 2:8, 14-17; 1 John 3:16-17; 4:11).

The Law of the Spirit (5:16-24)

In the final verses of this section Paul focuses on the concrete results of being free in the Spirit. Freedom does not mean the liberty to do anything or everything. Even without the law there has to be discipline. Even Christians who are guided by God's powerful Spirit and have good intentions are still subject to temptations. Even those who try to follow Christ can be led astray and wander off the path.

Paul urges his readers, therefore, to walk by the Spirit. Walking by the Spirit does not lead to the restrictions and constraints of the law. Instead, it is similar to Robert Frost's description of the rules of poetry, which allow freedom of movement and freedom to be creative, "riding easy in harness." The Christian is freed from the shackles of the law, to be sure, but willingly submits to the guidance of the Spirit to continue on the track Christ has laid out.

Walking was a term used by both Jews and Gentiles to describe a religious or ethical way of life, and Paul employs it often to describe Christian living (Romans 8:4;

2 Corinthians 5:7). It is similar to the idea of "following" Jesus, which describes the Christian faith as an exciting pilgrimage behind the Lord of life (see Mark 1:18; 2:14, 15; 5:24; 6:1; 8:34; 10:21, 28, 32, 52, for examples).

The words *the desires of the flesh* in verses 16 and 17 describe the struggle which Paul and all Christians undergo as they try to keep their lives in line with God's direction. As Jesus said, the spirit is willing, but the flesh, human nature, is weak (Matthew 26:41). Paul admits as much in Romans 7:14-21 where he candidly describes the difficult battle between desire and performance.

The Spirit and the flesh are opposed. It is that simple. So Christians must be careful to walk only in the Spirit. In order to help that take place, Paul lists the habits and the attitudes that the flesh encourages and the ones that walking in the Spirit produces.

In verses 18-23 a catalogue of Christian virtues and vices is listed to help the Galatians live a Christian life. Such catalogues were very familiar to Jews and Gentiles alike, and were a popular way of giving moral teaching. Other examples in the New Testament are found in Romans 1:29-31; 13:12-13; Ephesians 5:1-20; Colossians 3:5-17; 2 Timothy 3:2-5; Mark 7:21-23.

The list of vices (verse 19) begins with special attention to sexual indiscretions. Acts 15:20 indicates that at the Jerusalem Conference (see the discussion above of Galatians 2), it was recognized that sexual immorality was a particular problem for Gentiles.

Fornication refers to unlawful sexual intercourse, generally between persons who are unmarried (see 1 Corinthians 6:18; 1 Thessalonians 4:3-8). In ancient Greek, *impurity* originally described the uncleanness of an open wound. In the New Testament it often refers to moral depravity or ceremonial impurity (Matthew 23:27). For Paul it has to do with sexual looseness (Romans 1:24; 6:19; 2 Corinthians 12:21).

Licentiousness is another term for sexual license. It can also mean *wantonness, violence,* or *lewdness* (Mark 7:22; Romans 13:13, 14; 2 Corinthians 12:20-21; 2 Peter 2:2, 7, 18).

Idolatry is a Jewish term that describes the worship of Gentile gods (1 Corinthians 10:14; 1 Peter 4:3; see Galatians 4:8).

Sorcery means the practice of magic, witchcraft, and particularly the use of drugs, potions, or spells to create a mood or a religious experience. Paul warns the Galatians that they should only get high on the Spirit. For references to the danger of sorcery see Acts 8:9-13; 13:8-12; 19:13-20.

Enmity is the opposite of love; it is the opposite of peace. In its basic form it refers to party spirit (Luke 23:12), or to hostility to God (Romans 8:7; Ephesians 2:14, 16; James 4:4). Possibly Paul means the basic rebellion against God, which is the chief characteristic of sin.

Strife also means *contention, competition for honor,* or *quarreling.* Paul frequently warns against it, probably because he had experienced its devasting effects both outside and inside the church (Romans 1:29; 1 Corinthians 1:11; 3:3).

Jealousy (*zealos* in Greek)—in the New Testament this word can mean *zeal* (John 2:17; Romans 10:2; 2 Corinthians 7:7; Philippians 3:6); *anger* (Acts 5:17; 13:45; Hebrews 10:27) or *jealousy* (Romans 13:13; 1 Corinthians 3:3; James 3:14, 16).

Anger means *hostile feelings* that people have toward one another or toward God (Luke 4:28; Acts 19:28; 2 Corinthians 12:20; Ephesians 4:31; Colossians 3:8; Hebrews 11:27).

It is not certain what the Greek word translated in the Revised Standard Version as *selfishness* really means. In the Greek it can also mean *strife* or *contention,* especially in the seeking of political office. It may have one of those meanings in Galatians, too, where Paul is warning about the opposition against him, people who are seeking power in the church (see Romans 2:8, *factious*; Philippians 1:17, *partisanship*).

Dissension also has a political or military meaning. It can signify *treason* or *sedition*. See Romans 16:17, *take note of those who create dissensions and difficulties*.

Party spirit generally refers to political groups or parties, religious sects, or schools of religion. In Acts (5:17; 15:5; 26:5) it refers to sects within Judaism. Acts 24:5 refers to Christianity as the *Nazarene* party. It can also mean *faction* (Acts 24:14; 1 Corinthians 11:19).

Envy means *ill-will* or *malice*. It is similar to jealousy (see Matthew 27:18; Mark 15:10; Romans 1:29). Paul warns in Philippians 1:15 that some of his opponents preach Christ out of envy.

Paul concludes the list with warnings against drunkenness and carousing (see Luke 21:34; Romans 13:13; Ephesians 5:18; 1 Peter 4:3). The sober reminder that those who walk in the flesh will never inherit the kingdom of God seems harsh (see the discussion of 4:1-7), but similar admonitions are found in 1 Corinthians 6:9 and 15:50. Also see Ephesians 5:5. It implies that those who live in such a way have *severed* (Galatians 5:4) themselves from Christ so much by ignoring the Spirit that they cannot be his anymore. Biblical scholars suggest that the expression *inherit the kingdom* may have been used regularly in baptismal services or in the reception of new members, and may have been familiar to the Galatians through their own services of worship.

In verses 22-24 Paul turns from the negative to the positive, from life outside the Spirit to the fruit of the Spirit. The language here is connected with church life. The vocabulary of the church is also that of the Holy Spirit.

Fruit of the Spirit refers to the idea that in the Spirit the Christian is constantly growing and producing for God's kingdom. It is possible that the language entered the church from the Old Testament (see Psalm 1:3; Proverbs 1:31; 8:19; 11:30; Jeremiah 21:14). It may also have come from Jesus' references to the vine and the branches (John 15:5, 8, 16). Possibly the idea is present that the Holy Spirit plants the seeds in the spirit of the believers and they produce spiritual "fruit" for God. The image of the spiritual fruit is a common one in the New Testament (Matthew 7:15-20; Luke 3:8; 8:15; Romans 7:4; Philippians 1:11; Colossians 1:10; Hebrews 12:11). Many of the qualities included here in Galatians are available to Christians because they are fundamental qualities of God, the one who gives them.

For *love* see the discussion of 5:6, 13-14.

Joy is a feeling that comes from being close to God and being part of God's plan. It is a response in the Gospels, for example, to Jesus' miraculous birth (Matthew 2:10; Luke 1:14; 2:10) and later to his ministry (Luke 6:22-23; 10:17). Paul connects it with hope (Romans 12:12 and 15:13) and the power of the Holy Spirit (Philippians 2:1-4). He often mentions joy as a constant of the Christian life, even in the midst of great suffering, pain and persecution, since the Holy Spirit brings hope, peace, and comfort (see 2 Corinthians 2:3; 7:4, 13). Joy is a spiritual fruit Christians may search for and request from God (Psalm 51:11-12).

For *peace* see the discussion of 1:3.

Patience also means *steadfastness, endurance,* or *forebearance.* It points to patience toward God or toward other people. It was considered to be a characteristic of Christ and his servants (2 Corinthians 6:6; Colossians 1:11; 2 Peter 3:15). It can also describe God's own patience (Romans 2:4; 9:22; 1 Timothy 1:16; 1 Peter 3:20). Second Timothy 3:10 says that it was particularly a strong point of Paul's.

The basic meaning of *kindness* is *goodness, uprightness,* or *generosity.* It is a characteristic of God (Romans 2:4; 11:22; Titus 3:4). *Goodness* is similar but can also mean *excellence* or *honesty*. It is a fruit of light (Ephesians 5:9), and something which the Christian can expect through the power of the Spirit (Romans 15:14). Christians, Paul seems to be saying, are easy to spot, because they are kind and gentle people.

Faithfulness does not refer to one's beliefs, but to a basic characteristic of fidelity or trustworthiness (see Matthew 23:23; Romans 3:3; Titus 2:10). The Christian is constant in faithfulness to God and God's ways.

Gentleness comes from the same Greek word that is translated as *meek* in Matthew 5:5, *blessed are the meek*. In the ancient world *meek* had the meaning *tamed*, and often referred to wild horses that had been trained. Paul may have that image in mind as he thinks of the Christian having all of the wild desires and passions in 5:19-21 tamed under the direction of the Spirit. The same idea is found in Matthew 11:29, where Jesus says, *Take my yoke upon you*. Under Christ the "wild beast" in us becomes gentle and lowly of heart, fit for God's service. Also see Galatians 6:1; Ephesians 4:2; Colossians 3:12; Titus 3:2; 1 Peter 3:15.

The final word in the Spirit-fruit list is *self-control*. Usually it was used in the ancient world in reference to sexual matters (see 1 Corinthians 7:9). It is just the opposite of the first three vices listed in 5:18. It also had the more general meaning of being spiritually disciplined (Acts 24:25; 1 Corinthians 9:25; Titus 1:8).

Paul concludes his catalogue by saying, rather facetiously, *against such there is no law*. Whereas there are laws against the vices listed in Galatians 5 in almost all cultures and religions, no one would make regulations against the fruits of the Spirit. They are all lawful and good, and the Christian has complete freedom to pursue them. Paul summarizes the concept of freedom with his favorite image of having the sinful self crucified with Christ and the new Spirit-filled Christian rising to new life. See the discussion of 2:20-21 and 3:13 above.

§ § § § § § §

The Message of Galatians 5

§ In the fifth chapter Paul provides moral advice (exhortation) to his readers and gives some practical examples of how they should live.

§ He repeats his understanding of circumcision: Those who practice it are obligated to keep the whole law. Since it is impossible for anyone to be that good, those who try are cut off from Christ. By returning to Christ through the Spirit, the Christian may have hope again.

§ The chief characteristic of the Christian faith is not one of restriction but of freedom. Freedom comes from the gift of the Holy Spirit, especially the gift of love which allows a person to give himself or herself away to God and to others.

§ The walk with the Spirit is a pilgrimage on the road that has been designed for those who follow God. Paul concludes with those things that do not characterize a person led by the Spirit and those that do.

§ § § § § § §

PART EIGHT Galatians 6:1-10

Introduction to These Verses

In this section of his letter Paul turns from the characteristics of individuals to those of the church. These verses briefly summarize how Christians are to behave toward other people, particularly those in the church, in the household of faith (6:10).

Some Practical Examples (6:1-10)

Paul begins by saying that if we live by the Spirit, let us also walk by the Spirit. The word for *walk* in Greek here is not the same one used in 5:16. Instead, this word is a military term which indicates that the Christian should form up, get in line, and count off to form a united front with other Christians. The same word is used in 6:16, *walk by this rule*. Many times Paul has used military terms in Galatians to indicate that the Christian life is a battle (2:12; 5:1, 13-15, 20). Here he argues that if people really are made alive by God's Spirit, they ought to act like it and work together for God's kingdom (see Romans 4:12, *follow*; Philippians 3:16, *hold true*). The same term is used in Hellenistic writings to refer to following a philosopher's principles. Here it is the Spirit, and ultimately Christ, who is the believer's leader. The results of this forming up involve responsibilities toward oneself and toward the neighbor, reponsibilities that allow the church to operate in love. Anyone who has ever served in a church can read 6:1-10 and see more than general instructions. Personalities appear of people who have served on church committees or denominational boards. Members with great personal needs, who require special care, can be visualized. Discussions about the proper support of pastors in congregational meetings can be recalled which make it very clear what Paul is talking about here.

Paul begins by urging each reader to know himself or herself before turning to others in the congregation. The basic principle is one of agape love. There should be no power plays, no concern about one's own importance, no desire to get another member's goat (5:25). Those who live and work in the everyday world of the church know how difficult it is to prevent these things; it is only possible if the Spirit intervenes.

A basic principle is stated in 6:2-4: Each person has to look for the beam in his or her own eye before criticizing a brother or sister in faith. The appeal to *know thyself* is a well-known theme in Greek literature, especially in the teaching of Socrates, and is important in any community where some people have authority over others. Throughout this section Paul uses ideas that were familiar to those acquainted with Hellenistic philosophy, and he adapts them to the Christian lifestyle.

In 6:1 he begins to discuss some of the responsibilities that Christians have toward one another. He refers to the Galatians in complimentary terms here, as spiritual people, assuming that the fruit of the Spirit is already in them (see the discussion of 3:5 above).

One of the duties of spiritual leaders is to correct those who are overtaken in a sin (perhaps those listed in 5:18-21?) and restore them in gentleness (see 5:23). How this was done, whether it was casually or through some form of church discipline (see Matthew 18:15-20; James 5:19-20), is not said. What is clear is that its purpose is to bring the offender back into the fellowship of the church.

Bear one another's burdens (verse 2) is a common proverb about friendship in the Greek world. The burdens are the problems Christians face in their daily lives. Christian community is marked by care and concern expressed for other members when they are in need. It is a response to God's willingness to bear our burdens (Psalm 55:22). It is a fulfillment of the law because it is putting the second law of love into practice (Galatians 5:14).

Verse 5, *each man will have to bear his own load*, is not a contradiction to the advice to bear one another's burdens in verse 2. In verse 5 Paul refers to the fact that we must all stand on our own before God. Each person must test his or her own work to make sure that God's commands are being lived out.

The same idea is contained in verses 7-9, where Paul uses a picture from farm life. Reaping and sowing are common images all through the Bible (see Job 4:8; Psalm 126:5; Proverbs 22:8; Mark 4:1-20; 2 Corinthians 9:6), and here it is a warning about God's judgment in the final days. If anyone plants seeds like those listed in 5:18-22, the result will be death. Those who produce fruit of the Spirit will have eternal life.

Let him who is taught the word share all good things with him who teaches (verse 6) is a basic principle of stewardship in the church. Paul and others like him were entitled to support by members of the church, and fair support at that (1 Corinthians 9:12-14).

Verse 10 summarizes the attitude which Christians should have toward one another. They should do good to all people, especially those in the church. The doing is not the works of the law, but the production of the fruit of the Spirit in 5:22.

The phrase *household of faith* is a good metaphor for the church (see Ephesians 2:19). It describes the closeness of the congregation as a family where people are accepted and loved for what they are. It also hints that Paul knows that the very things that he warns against in 6:1-6 do happen in the church. Thus Paul reminds the Galatians in 6:10 that it is sometimes hardest to get along with those who are part of the same family. *Household* may also reflect the fact that the early Christians often did not have church buildings but literally did meet in the houses of members (Acts 12:12; 1 Corinthians 16:19). The word *house* is also a common metaphor for the place where God is worshiped (2 Samuel 7:11; 2 Chronicles 5:14; Psalm 122:1; Matthew 21:13).

§ § § § § § §

The Message of Galatians 6:1-10

§ Paul turns in this section to a practical working out of the fruit of the Spirit in the Christian congregation.

§ In order to march in line in the Spirit (5:25), Christians need to keep in mind certain responsibilities to each other. These include correcting each other's faults, bearing other members' burdens, and sharing with teachers and pastors.

§ Paul also warns that each Christian must examine himself or herself as an individual before taking on responsibilities in the church. Each person will get the fruit he or she has sowed, either for evil or for good. Christians should seek only to do good to all people, especially to other believers.

§ § § § § § §

PART
NINE **Galatians 6:11-18**

Introduction to These Verses

Paul concludes Galatians with personal words and a summary of some of the main themes of the letter.

My Own Signature (6:11)

He begins the final section with a comment about his own writing. Although a secretary has transcribed the letter that Paul has been dictating (see Romans 16:22; 1 Corinthians 16:21; Colossians 4:18 for other examples), Paul writes a few lines himself so that the Galatians can know that it really comes from him. Perhaps he has made some kind of special mark to insure that it is authentic (2 Thessalonians 3:17). In any case, his handwriting is so large, probably because of poor eyesight, that it is easily recognizable. For a discussion of the problems Paul had with his eyes see comments on 4:12-15.

Walk in the Shadow of the Cross (6:12-16)

In verses 12-13 Paul attacks his opponents one last time. His enemies want to have the Galatian Christians circumcised only so they do not have to be persecuted themselves. By preaching a gospel that is based on the Jewish law and its traditions, they do not have to worry about the opposition of Jewish Christians or the hatred of the Jews as Paul does. According to Acts, Paul's Jewish opponents hounded him constantly about his teaching concerning Jesus' death and resurrection, managed to have him arrested and, as later tradition tells us, finally executed. The people who oppose him are like the hypocrites Jesus mentions in Matthew 23:23. They boast about their ability to lay the law on others but do not intend to keep it themselves.

Paul struggles in his ministry to avoid all boasting whatsoever, although it is easy to suppose that for someone with such a strong ego, someone so sure of himself, it was a daily battle. He has decided that if he is to do any boasting at all it will only be in God and God's grace (1 Corinthians 1:31; 2 Corinthians 11:16–12:13). Although philosophers and Jewish and Christian teachers may have built up their own reputations by boasting about their own achievements, Paul knows that those who think they are something on the basis of their own merit are only fooling themselves (6:3-5). Paul rests his case in Christ and his cross. All his worldly desires to look out only for himself have died in them. Now he is only interested in Christ and his church.

All of the debate and discussion about circumcision and uncircumcision, Paul finally admits, really amounts to nothing. What really counts is the *new creation* (verse 15) in Christ. The new creation is the new life *in Christ* (2:20). It is the end of reliance on the old ways of Judaism. It is the end of belief in elemental spirits (4:3, 9). It is the end of faith in false gods (4:8). It is the end of a life ruled by evil (5:17-21), and it is the end of selfishness (5:14-15; 6:3-5, 7-10). The new creation is so exciting and so fresh and so different that the Christian may feel as though life has been started all over again. This is the end of old habits and old religions and the creation of a new people and new systems of belief in Christ Jesus. As Paul says in 2 Corinthians 5:17-18, *If anyone is in Christ Jesus, he is a new creation; the old has passed away, behold the new has come. All this is from God, who through Christ reconciled us to himself and gave us the ministry of reconciliation.*

This section ends with an unusual statement that has caused much discussion among biblical scholars. Unlike the benediction in verse 18, the blessing in verse 16 is different from those Paul uses to close other letters. It appears to be a quotation from an ancient prayer used in Jewish services of worship. The words there are very similar to the Blessing of Peace: *Bestow peace, happiness and blessing, grace and loving-kindness and mercy upon us and all Israel, your people.* But why would Paul quote a Jewish tradition when he has been arguing against such things for six chapters? Possibly it is his last and rather unkind dig against his opponents. By quoting their own prayer back to them he disposes of them once and for all. The ancient blessing of God no longer belongs to them but can only be claimed by those who march in line (see 5:25) with the measure or rule (*kanon* in Greek) that Paul has established in his letter.

The *Israel of God* may be understood in the same light. Here he is not talking about the Jewish nation favored by God in the Old Testament. As he says in Romans 2:28-29, the real Israel, the real Jewish people, is made up of those who obey God inwardly, spiritually, from the heart. For Paul, the real Israel is made up of the Christian church, those who are living in God's new plan for humanity through Christ (see Romans 9:6-8). Perhaps Paul borrowed the expression *Israel of God* from his opponents, who used it to describe themselves. To them Paul's parting words are, "You are not the true Israel at all, and the ancient blessings apply to you no more." As he says in Philippians 3:3, *For we are the true circumcision, who worship God in Spirit, and glory in Christ Jesus, and put no confidence in the flesh.*

I Bear the Marks of Jesus (6:17)

Paul finishes his arguments with a personal comment. His opponents can leave him alone from now on. If his reasoning does not persuade them, his bruises should. *For I bear on my body the marks of Jesus.* The Greek word which Paul uses for marks is *stigmata*. Stigmata were tattoos that owners branded on slaves to make sure they could not escape. They were also religious brands which people put on themselves to show that they were committed to a particular pagan god or goddess. Sometimes soldiers even burned a mark on themselves to indicate their army regiment or commander. Paul, of course, did not have tattoos on his body, but he did have scars from his beatings and imprisonments (2 Corinthians 11:23-25). Paul is marked by his loyalty to Christ. Christ is his master, his Lord, and his commander-in-chief.

The Benediction (6:18)

Paul ends his letter with words similar to those with which he started in 1:3, *the grace of our Lord Jesus Christ be with your spirit. Amen.* He hopes that the human spirit of his readers will be made one with the love and forgiveness of Christ and the freedom of God's Holy Spirit. *Amen* is a traditional ending of a Jewish prayer, meaning *so be it*. So, Paul prays, may the truth of Christ be with all who read this letter. Amen.

§ § § § § § §

The Message of Galatians 6:11-18

§ Paul concludes his letter by writing the last few lines in his own handwriting. This action enables his readers to know that he wrote the letter. It also gives him an opportunity to express his last thoughts more personally.

§ The main argument of the letter (verses 12-16) is that Paul's opponents are not telling the truth about the law. Real life comes from Christ and his cross. Those who believe in him will have new life.

§ The letter ends as it began (1:3). Paul prays that the free gift of Christ in love may be with all of his readers.

§ § § § § § §

Introduction to Ephesians

Who Wrote Ephesians?

It is nearly impossible to begin a discussion of Ephesians without looking first at the question of authorship. For over 150 years there has been a continuous, sustained debate about the real author of Ephesians, and that debate continues. Some scholars take what the letter says at face value and assume that because Paul is mentioned by name in 1:1 and 3:1 that the apostle Paul must be the author. Many others argue that because of the style, content, and perspective of the letter someone other than Paul must surely have written it.

All serious students of Ephesians agree that the letter presents difficult problems. The content differs particularly from Romans and Galatians and clearly has different major themes. Whereas justification by faith, freedom from the law, and the question of circumcision are primary issues in Romans and Galatians, they are not of first importance in Ephesians. Ephesians, moreover, has unbearably long and complex sentences. Although Paul sometimes uses a lengthy style (see Romans 1:1-7 which is one sentence), generally he does not, and certainly not page after page.

The author of Ephesians also indicates a very reverential attitude toward the apostles, which differs considerably from that in Galatians 1 and 2 (see the Introduction to Galatians above), and many scholars are convinced that Paul could not have changed his mind so much in a relatively short time.

Those who think that Paul wrote Ephesians argue that it is not unusual for authors to change their style if they are writing at different times in their lives for different readers. In addition, they point out, there are themes in Ephesians which are found throughout Paul's other genuine letters. In their opinion, Paul's style may differ in Ephesians because he is older and because he quotes more Christian hymns and Old Testament Scriptures in that letter.

While these arguments are worth considering, it is most likely, as most scholars argue, that Paul did not write Ephesians. The long, ponderous style is different from his writings anywhere else in the New Testament. The attitude toward the apostles is also very revealing. In Galatians 1:16 Paul says that he did not have to confer with other apostles (*flesh and blood*) to receive revelation from God, and refers to them as *those who were reputed to be something*, who added nothing to him (2:6).

In Ephesians, however, the apostles are people who should be honored. Although the Spirit has revealed the mystery to *his holy apostles and prophets* (3:5), and the church was built on them (2:20), the author implies that they were people who received a blessing from God in the past and that he himself was not one of them. It is also unlikely that Paul would call himself a "holy" apostle. In 1 Corinthians 15:8-10 he refers to himself instead as one *untimely born*, as one of *the least of the apostles*.

For these and other reasons, it is best to assume that Ephesians was written not during Paul's lifetime, but much later, when the church was an established institution that revered the apostles as figures of the past.

Who wrote the letter then? Over the centuries many suggestions have been made, but it is most likely that Ephesians was written by an unknown Christian who borrowed Paul's name. Perhaps he was a student of Paul's or, more probably, an admirer who respected his memory as a "holy apostle."

In the ancient world it was not unusual for a writer to assume another's name if he thought that the author's ideas were similar to his. It is likely that the New Testament books of James and Jude were written the same way, utilizing the names of apostles to make sure that the letters were widely read.

In a final sense, it may not be critically important who wrote Ephesians. The author of Hebrews is also unknown, but all Christians realize that it contains Christian truth. In a similar way, Ephesians has a great deal to teach us about Christ's church, the unity of his body, and the way Christians should act.

To Whom Was the Letter Written?

We cannot be certain where the original readers of Ephesians lived. The oldest and most reliable copies of Ephesians do not contain any reference at all to those *who are at Ephesus* (see footnote *a* in the Revised Standard Version). Moreover, the writer indicates that he does not know his readers (1:15; 3:2-3; 4:21), whereas the apostle Paul was very friendly with them, having conducted a three-year ministry in their city (Acts 18:19-21; 19:1-20; 20:17-38). It is possible, as is often suggested, that Ephesians was a "circular letter" that left the name of the recipients blank and was sent around to many different churches in one area. Although we cannot be certain, it is likely that the letter was sent to congregations throughout western Asia Minor (modern Turkey).

Why Was the Letter Written?

In a strict sense, Ephesians is not a letter, but a style of writing called *rhetoric* in the ancient world. Rhetoric was delivered in speeches or written in tracts to influence the thought and conduct of a general audience. Unlike Paul's letters, Ephesians is not directed toward incidents in a specific church, but is written very generally to build the Christian church as a whole (Chapters 1–3) and tell the readers how they should act (Chapters 4–6).

The author's writing indicates that his readers are aware of a popular philosophy which was called *Gnosticism*. He appears to be worried that they may be influenced by it so much that they might lose their faith in Christ because of it. Gnosticism was a philosophy which prided itself on the knowledge (*gnosis* in Greek) of those who believed in it. In one popular form of the belief system, followers believed that only they could understand the mystery (see 3:3) of the unknowable God. They thought that there was a whole series of planets and beings in different levels of heaven that controlled human destiny. Sometimes they were given names like *princes of the air* (*archons* in Greek, 2:2), *ages* (*aeons*, see 3:9), *principalities*, and *powers* (3:10). The goal of philosophy and religion, in their opinion, was to return the divine spark that dwells in every human being to the fullness of God in the highest heaven (3:19), so that all divine things could be all in all.

The writer of Ephesians counters this kind of thinking with the Christian belief that through Christ, God has overcome all heavenly beings, real or unreal. All things will rest in God who brings the love that surpasses all knowledge.

Ephesians is written to Gentiles, that is, to people who were not born as Jews (see 3:1, *you Gentiles*; 3:8). The writer refers to them as aliens and strangers (2:12), those who were once far off (2:13, 17), in order to show them that in Christ their status has been changed and they are now part of the one body of Christ (2:14-18), fellow citizens in the household of God (2:19).

When Was Ephesians Written?

Ephesians was written sometime after Paul's death in A.D. 64-67 (the exact year is not known) and the end of the first century. Since reference is made to it in a letter written about A.D. 96 to Christians in Rome by the first bishop of that city (Clement I), it is often assumed that Ephesians was completed sometime around A.D 90.

PART TEN Ephesians 1:1-2

Introduction to These Verses

In these first two verses we encounter the writer of the letter. See the introduction to Ephesians for more information concerning this individual.

Greetings (1:1-2)

Ephesians begins with the traditional formula for greetings in ancient letters: the identification of the writer and the recipients, followed by words of good will. (See the first verses of other letters in the New Testament and the discussion of Galatians 1:1-5 above.) As has already been indicated in the Introduction, the apostle Paul probably did not write Ephesians. Someone else who used his name composed it many years after his death.

The word *apostle* means *one who is sent*. It is discussed in detail in reference to Galatians 1:1 and 1:11-15 above.

The author of Ephesians indicates that his calling as an apostle is through the will of God. Throughout the letter he returns to this thought to indicate that everything that happens to Christians is caused by God's plan and choice (see 1:5, 9, 11; 5:17). In Chapter 1 he makes it clear that all things take place according to God's purpose (verses 9, 10), God's plan (verse 10), and the counsel of God's will (verse 11). Things in heaven and earth are not directed by chance or by other heavenly beings; they are all in accord with the eternal purpose which God has realized in Christ Jesus (3:11). See the discussion of Galatians 1:15-16 for the apostle Paul's understanding of how God directs individuals to do God's work.

The writer refers to his readers as *saints*. This word does not mean that they have earned some special status in the church, but that they are *holy* or *sanctified* or *set apart* by God for a particular use in God's kingdom. In Ephesians the word is synonymous with *Christian* (1:15; 2:19; 3:8,18; 4:12; 5:3; 6:18).

Faithful in Christ (1:1) refers to those who are unshakable and consistent in their belief in Jesus as the messiah expected by the people of Israel. Faithfulness is listed in Galatians 5:22 as a fruit of the Holy Spirit.

In Christ is a favorite expression of the Ephesians author and occurs more than thirty times throughout the letter. It describes a special closeness that a believer can have to Jesus, one that is so intimate that it is closer than one's own skin. In just the first two chapters the writer uses this word to describe how God does everything through Christ's agency. God blesses (1:3), chooses believers (1:4), sets forth the divine purpose (1:9), unites all things (1:10), communicates the word of truth (1:13), works great might (1:19-20), raises believers up from the dead (2:5-6), shows the immeasurable richness of God's grace (2:7), and creates Ephesians' readers for good works (2:10), all in Christ. See the discussion of Galatians 2:20 for the apostle Paul's use of the same expression.

The words *grace, peace,* and *Father* are all defined in reference to Galatians 1:3.

Lord in Ephesians 1:2 is a title of honor that was commonly used in the ancient world. It could refer to a king, an emperor, a landowner, a slavemaster (6:5), or an employer. In the Old Testament it is often used as a title for God. Recent discoveries demonstrate that Jews who lived by the Dead Sea also referred to God as "the Lord". In the New Testament Jesus is considered to be the Lord above all other lords, whether they are emperors or other gods or goddesses (Acts 2:34-36; 11:20; 1 Corinthians 8:6; 9:14; Philippians 2:11). The first Christians used the prayer "our Lord, come" (*maranatha*) to describe their faith that Jesus would return in power at the end of history (1 Corinthians 16:22; Revelation 22:20). In Ephesians *Lord* describes Jesus more than twenty times. All things are summed up in the *Lord* (4:5), and the letter ends with reference to him (6:23-24).

§ § § § § § §

The Message of Ephesians 1:1-2

§ In the first two verses of Chapter 1 the author of Ephesians introduces himself and identifies himself as an apostle. He is called by the will of God and his readers are called saints because they also are set apart for God's special purpose.

§ *In Christ* refers to the special closeness that those faithful to him can experience, a spiritual intimacy that indicates that all of God's purpose is realized in him.

§ In these verses the writer greets his readers with a typical Christian blessing, extending to them God's special gift in Christ and the peacefulness that comes only from God.

§ § § § § § §

Ephesians 1:3-14

Introduction to These Verses

Ephesians 1:3 begins one of the longest sentences in the New Testament. In the Greek, it extends from verse 3 all the way through verse 14! Because of this kind of style the writer of Ephesians has often been accused of writing nearly incomprehensible sentences, connected only by the barest threads of logic. But even though Ephesians is not easy to understand, if the words are allowed to flow as if they were cascading from a wonderfully refreshing waterfall, the pattern of thought becomes very clear. The message is that all things in heaven and on earth have been planned by God in Christ according to God's good will.

Blessed by God (1:3)

In verse 3 the writer begins with a blessing or benediction given to the God who blesses him and his readers. With the words *blessed be*, *blessed us* and *every spiritual blessing* he opens his letter with a typical Jewish form of prayer or praise called a *berakah*. This type of praise occurs frequently in the Old Testament and usually begins *Blessed be God* or *Blessed be the Lord* (Psalm 41:13; 66:20; 72:18). Christians used it in their own way by including the name of Jesus (2 Corinthians 1:3-4; 1 Peter 1:3). In its most basic form, *bless* means *to praise* or *glorify* when it is given by human beings to God, and *to give benefits* or *to protect* when it is something God does for those who believe. The spiritual blessings that God gives to the people include being called in God's love (1:5), redemption (1:7), God's plan to unite all things in Christ (1:10), the gift of the Holy Spirit (1:13), and the inheritance as God's children (1:14). For a discussion of the concept of blessing and cursing in the Bible see the comments on Galatians 3:8-9 above.

The spiritual blessings that God offers include all of those that are available in the heavenly places. Here the *heavens* refers to the spiritual realm where the angels and other spiritual beings dwell. It is possible that the writer is thinking of the picture of heaven assumed by those who believed in some form of gnostic thought (see the Introduction, "Why Was The Letter Written?"). In 2 Corinthians 12:2 Paul indicates that he knew that there were several levels of heavens. In Ephesians the author makes it clear that no matter where these heavens are or who lives in them, they are under the control of God in Christ (1:20-21; 2:6; 6:11-13). In 1:3, he promises his readers at the beginning that in spite of these evil forces, those who believe in Christ will still receive the spiritual blessings reserved for them in the heavenly places.

Chosen by God (1:4)

The blessings are available to Christians because this was God's plan from the very beginning, before the world was even formed. *Destined us in love* (verse 5) refers to the biblical concept of "election" in which God chooses those who will be obedient and faithful. For modern readers it is very difficult to understand how human beings can have free will and be held accountable for their actions if God chooses them and predestines their future. For the Jews, however, predestination was a necessity because they could not accept the possibility that things could happen solely by luck or human choice. Since God was all-powerful, all things had to be determined beforehand by God. God designated Israel to be the chosen people (Deuteronomy 7:7) and made the people of that nation God's heirs (Exodus 4:22; Jeremiah 31:20). If, as Colossians 1:16 says, all things were created by God in Christ, then it follows that God called all Christians from the very beginning. Jesus is the Chosen One, without equal (Luke 9:35; 23:35; John 1:34), and he is the one who chooses those who are to be his (John 15:16). In Ephesians 1:11-12 the writer once again says that Christians are destined and appointed according to the plan of God in Christ. (See Acts 13:17; 1 Corinthians 1:27-28; James 2:5; Romans 8:33 for references to election elsewhere in the New Testament.) For a discussion of the related idea of calling, see the comments on Galatians 1:6 and Ephesians 1:15 above.

Before the foundation of the earth refers to the time before there was any time, when God created the world and the cosmos in which it is placed. The Jews believed that God, as the Creator, had laid the foundations of the earth, which supported the rest of the superstructure of creation (see Genesis 1:1-10; Job 38:4; Psalm 102:25). Christians were sure that Christ, as the unique Son of God, was also present at Creation, and that it was through him that the world was made (John 1:1-4; 1 Corinthians 8:6; Colossians 1:15-20; Hebrews 1:3-4). As Colossians 1:16-17 puts it, *for in him all things were created, in heaven and on earth, visible and invisible, whether thrones or dominions or principalities or authorities—all things were created through him and for him. He is before all things, and in him all things hold together.*

It is this same Christ in Ephesians 1:4 who already chose those who would believe in him *before the foundation of the world.* The writer's concept here is similar to other New Testament passages where Christ chooses those who will follow him from the beginning. (See John 17:24; Matthew 25:34; 1 Peter 1:20; Revelation 13:8; 17:8.)

Holy is an adjective made from the same Greek root as the word *saints* in 1:1. To be holy means to be set apart for God, to be consecrated to God. Just as God is holy, that is, pure in all things (Exodus 15:11; Isaiah 1:4; 5:19;

6:3; Psalm 99), so those who are in Christ must also be holy (5:1-6; Colossians 1:22; Hebrews 12:14; 1 Peter 1:15-16). *Blameless* is a word that refers to the sacrificial systems in the ancient world in which spotless animals had to be presented to God or the gods in order for forgiveness to take place (see Numbers 6:14; 19:2). Since Jesus Christ's death on the cross is such a spotless sacrifice (Hebrews 9:14; 1 Peter 1:19), those who believe in him and have been redeemed by his blood (Ephesians 1:7) are also pure and spotless (Ephesians 5:27; Philippians 2:15; Colossians 1:22). Jude 24-25 summarizes many of the ideas contained in Ephesians 1:3-4.

Destined in Love (1:5-6)

Here the writer continues to develop his understanding of predestination. In verse 5 the words *He destined us in love to be his sons* could be translated more accurately *He predestined us for adoption through Jesus Christ.* The word for *destined* in this verse is similar in meaning to *chose* in verse 4. It means *decide beforehand.* Thus in Acts 4:28 the same word is used when it is said that all of the evil things that happened to Jesus were predestined by God as part of the divine plan for salvation. Paul expresses the way this works for individual believers in Romans 8:28-30, when he says that all things work for good for those predestined to be God's children.

God's choosing beforehand of those who will believe in Christ is not a coldblooded plan, but one that is based on God's love for the chosen people. For a detailed discussion of the New Testament concept of adoption see the comments on Galatians 3:26 and 4:1-7.

Destined in love refers to the generous, self-giving love of God found in Jesus Christ. It is the love called *agape* in Greek, the love which Paul describes so eloquently in 1 Corinthians 13, that which is open and forgiving. Its definition and nature are discussed above in reference to Galatians 5:6, 14, and 22.

In Ephesians 1:6 the writer says that God's love is best expressed in Jesus Christ, so much so that he is called the *beloved* or *one who is loved*. See Colossians 1:13; Mark 1:11 and 9:7; and parallel passages in the other gospels where similar expressions are used. Since the love of God has been showered on Christ by God, those whom God chooses also receive the same love as adopted children. Since they have learned love from God, they must also give it to others (1 John 3:1-3, 23-24; 4:7-12; 5:1).

According to . . . his will in 1:5 refers to the concept prevalent in Ephesians that all things are done in concert with God's plan in Christ. (See the discussion of the word *will* in verse 1 above.) Here the Greek word that is used specifically means *good pleasure, favor* (Matthew 11:26; Luke 10:21), or *God's desire to provide good things or experiences to those whom he loves* (Luke 12:32).

Ephesians says that Christians are adopted by God's love. How does such a thing happen? The author simply says *through God's good will*. The word he uses is the same one used in the angels' song in the Christmas story in Luke's Gospel, sometimes translated, *Glory to God in the highest, and peace on earth, good will toward men*. How does God adopt believers as children? Through his good pleasure, through the gift of God's nature, through the divine grace in Christ. Why does God do it? Because of love for the chosen people. But why does God love them? As Martin Luther once said, "God's love has no why." It is God's nature.

The words *to the praise of his glorious grace* sum up the writer's understanding of God's love in Christ. It is a wonderful thing, almost beyond understanding, and it can only lead to a hymn of praise (see 1:12, 14).

Redeemed Through Christ (1:7-8)

The author of Ephesians begins this section with the seemingly insignificant *In him*. But like the expression *in Christ*, these words capsulize his understanding of how all things are wrapped up in heaven and earth in God's plan in Christ. In verses 7-13, the three major sections begin with the words *In him. In him we have redemption through his blood and the forgiveness of sins* (1:7). *In him we have been called according to the counsel of his will* (1:11). *In him you have also heard the word of truth* (1:13).

In verse 7 *redemption* refers to the release of an object or person in exchange for some kind of payment. (See the comments on Galatians 3:10-14 above.) The same word is used in Ephesians 4:30.

Forgiveness of our trespasses is a description of the abolishment of the penalty for sin through the death of Jesus on the cross. *Trespasses* can also be translated *sins*. Sin is any human action that results in the disobedience of God's commands or will. In essence it means "a missing of the mark." Paul usually understands sin as that one thing so tragic that it alienates humanity from God and leads to physical and spiritual death (Romans 3:9, 20; 5:12-13; Chapters 6–8; 2 Corinthians 5:21). Even though the writer of Ephesians only uses it in the plural, he appears to give it the same strong and serious meaning (see 2:1, 5).

According to the riches of his grace which he lavished upon us is a good example of the effusive language which the author of Ephesians likes to use. It indicates that the gift of love in Christ is much more than could ever be expected or imagined and is absolutely wonderful. In other verses he speaks of *the riches of his glorious inheritance* (1:18), *the immeasurable richness of his grace in kindness* (2:7), *the unsearchable riches of Christ* (3:8) and *the riches of his glory* (3:16). Truly, for this writer, the power of God in Christ is far more abundant than all we can ask or think (3:20). (See Romans 2:4; 9:23; 11:33.)

United in Christ (1:9-12)

Here the writer tells his readers that they are extremely blessed because God has made known to them, and to him (us), the mystery of the divine will in all wisdom and insight. Knowledge and wisdom are two of the most important themes in Ephesians, probably because the writer is reacting to the danger that gnostic ideas pose to his readers (see the Introduction above). Even though some people may think that they have special knowledge and insight into God's mysteries, the writer assures them that real knowledge is available only to those who know Jesus Christ. This mystery is one made known by God through revelation (3:3). It was not made known in the past to the Old Testament prophets, but it is now revealed to the apostles (3:5). In God's plan, this mystery is also being made known even in the heavenly places to the principalities and powers (3:10). Although it may be difficult to understand the complexity of the heavenly universe, and nearly impossible to probe God's nature, Ephesians assures believers that, in Christ, they will possess all the knowledge they could ever desire. This knowledge will help them comprehend *what is the breadth and length and height and depth, and to know the love of Christ which surpasses knowledge* (3:18-19). Similar ideas are presented in Colossians 1:27 and 2:2-3.

Wisdom is also an important theme in Ephesians. Certain parts of the Old Testament and the Apocrypha are referred to as Wisdom Literature because the concept of wisdom is so central in them (Proverbs, Job, Ecclesiastes, Wisdom of Jesus Ben Sirach, Wisdom of Solomon). In some passages, wisdom is described almost as if "she" were a living person or an extension of God (Proverbs 1:1-6; Chapters 2–4; 8–9). In some gnostic systems, wisdom was a central feature. Sophia (the Greek word for *wisdom* is *sophia*) was one of the heavenly beings (principalities) and played a major part in salvation. In Ephesians, the writer tells his readers that wisdom is not an independent divine being, but is something completely under God's control. God gives it to believers in a spirit of revelation in the knowledge of Jesus Christ (1:17-18).

God does this only through the resurrection of Christ and by raising him to power over all powers and dominions (1:20-23). True wisdom is even made known to the principalities and powers in their heavenly places, and this is all part of the eternal purpose in Christ Jesus (3:10-11). (See Colossians 1:9, 28; 2:3; 3:16.)

Mystery is another word that was often used in the ancient world in religious circles. Many religions in the pagan world were called "mystery religions" because it was believed that the only people who understood the mysteries of the gods were those who had been initiated into them through certain religious rites. The New Testament warns against such practices (1 Corinthians 10:20). The Jews who lived in the Qumran area around the Dead Sea also spoke about the mysteries of God and how they were revealed to the community at large or to certain individuals within it. In Ephesians, the writer argues that the mystery (he only uses the word in the singular) of God is made known only in Jesus Christ (*the mystery of Christ*, 3:4). It is made known through his preaching (3:2-4). It is connected with God's creation and has been hidden for ages (see 1 Corinthians 2:6-7; Colossians 1:24-28) until it could be made known through the Christian church (3:9-10; see Mark 4:11; Colossians 4:3). It is the good news, the gospel, which is preached to and by those who believe in Christ (6:19). In essence, the mystery is Christ, his part in God's eternal plan, and the wonder of salvation brought by his death and resurrection (see Romans 16:25).

The use of the expression *the fulness of time* in verse 10 may also be a reaction to gnostic religious systems that threaten the beliefs of the readers of this letter. The Greek word for *fullness* could refer to the gnostic concept of the totality of God and the idea that at the end of time all things will be gathered into God (see the Introduction above). The writer says that there is only one way for time and history to be fulfilled, and that is through Jesus

Christ. It is not necessary to believe in pagan religions to have God's plan filled up; it will be done in Christ, who fills all in all (1:23). God will fill believers with this fullness, and this comes through the love of Christ (3:19). Christian maturity, which is being filled with the Holy Spirit (5:18), is the very fullness of Christ (4:13). Jesus Christ has been given power over all things and beings and he rules through the church, his body, which is the fullness of him who fills all in all. See Colossians 1:9; 2:9; and the discussion of Galatians 4:4 above.

For a discussion of the meaning of *unites all things in him* see the comments on 1:21-23 below.

Given the Guarantee of the Spirit (1:13-14)

In 1:13-14 the writer indicates that Gentile Christians can be sure that all things are filled up in Christ because they have been sealed with the promised Holy Spirit, which is the guarantee of our inheritance. In the ancient world a *seal* was a mark or impression put on a document that authenticated it. Usually it was an impression made on hot wax by a special stone that had an inscription etched on its surface. It could also be a symbol stamped on an object, which indicated who owned it. In the New Testament, the metaphor of the seal is used in a number of different ways. John guarantees that what he writes is true by setting his seal to it (John 3:33). God authenticates Jesus' ministry by putting a seal on him (John 6:27). Paul says that Abraham received circumcision as a seal of righteousness (Romans 4:11) . The Corinthians are the seal of his apostleship (1 Corinthians 9:2). It appears in the Book of Revelation many times (see 5:1, 2, 9; 6:1, 3, 5, 7, 9, 12; 7:2; 8:1; 9:4). In the early church, baptism was often considered to be the seal of the Spirit (2 Clement and the Shepherd of Hermas). In Ephesians, the writer indicates that the Holy Spirit confirms the salvation of his readers. He claims them for his own and seals them for the day of redemption (4:30). The Gentiles who are reading Ephesians can be sure that since they have been baptized and have received the gifts of the Holy Spirit (4:7-13), they will be fully incorporated into Christ's body (see Galatians 3:26-29).

Guarantee in 1:14 is an economic term for a deposit or down payment that was made to make sure that a buyer would pay the full price promised (see Genesis 38:17-18). The gift of the Holy Spirit is the guarantee that assures the Gentiles that they will gain possession of the inheritance that God has promised them, as soon as they are fulfilled in Christ and gain Christian maturity (2:7; 4:13). *He who has prepared us for this very thing is God, who has given us the Spirit as a guarantee* (2 Corinthians 5:5).

For *inheritance* see the comments on Galatians 4:1-17, 21-31 above.

For the meaning of the Holy Spirit see the discussion of Galatians 3:1-5.

$$\S\ \S\ \S\ \S\ \S\ \S\ \S$$

The Message of Ephesians 1:3-14

§ God has decided to focus the divine plan for salvation entirely in Christ Jesus.

§ God chose those who would be Christians before the foundation of the world and predestined them to be God's children.

§ In Christ is made known all wisdom and insight and the very mystery of God's plan for the whole universe.

§ Believers are assured that all things will be found in Christ. All things are sealed by the Holy Spirit, and believers are given a promise or guarantee that what God has promised will be delivered to them when they become mature Christians.

$$\S\ \S\ \S\ \S\ \S\ \S\ \S$$

Ephesians 1:15-23

Introduction to These Verses

The third section of Ephesians continues with the author's unusually lengthy sentence construction. Verses 15-23 have only two sentences in the original Greek, the first in verses 15-21 and the second in 22-23.

Thanks for Your Faith (1:15-18)

The author introduces this part with thanksgiving for the faith and love of his readers and with prayers for their continued spiritual welfare. Although the apostle Paul often begins his writings with similar introductions, he generally does so much earlier in the letter (see the opening verses of Romans, 1 Corinthians, Philippians, 1 and 2 Thessalonians, and Philemon).

Ephesians 1:15 is remarkably similar to Colossians 1:4, 9 in vocabulary and content. Indeed, the numerous similarities between the two letters have convinced most Bible scholars that the author of Ephesians had Colossians in hand when he wrote, and that he borrowed heavily from it. Further connections between the two epistles will be noted below.

The writer begins the section by thanking the readers for their faith in Jesus Christ and their love. He does so because he truly is thankful for their strengths as Christians, and also because he wants to compliment them and put them in a positive frame of mind so that they may receive and act on the criticisms and suggestions which he will make later.

The word *love* is not found in many reliable Greek manuscripts, and is possibly a later addition to the text (see footnote *c* in the Revised Standard Version). It may have been added to complete the famous trio of faith, hope, and love (1 Corinthians 13:13).

Although the writer does not know his readers personally, he wants them to understand that he feels close to them and that he is remembering them in his prayers. He hopes that God will give them spiritual strength, and he reminds them that one of the duties of a pastor is to pray for the flock.

Father of glory is an unusual expression and appears in the New Testament only in this one place. In the Old Testament *glory* means *weight, importance,* or *value.* (See the discussion of Galatians 1:5 above.) Since, for Christians, Jesus Christ is the main sign of God's importance and value for the world (Colossians 1:27), God then becomes the Father of glory. The word is also used in Ephesians 1:6, 12, 14, 18; 3:13, 16, 21.

In verse 17 the writer refers to the important concepts of wisdom, revelation, and knowledge that he has already mentioned in 1:9. By telling his readers that they have these gifts from God, he reminds them that they do not have to give in to those who practice other religions, those who argue that they have all wisdom and knowledge while Christians have none. The wisdom and knowledge of Christian believers come directly from God, and they are given through Jesus Christ. (See the discussion of 1:9 above.)

Seeing and not seeing, blindness and sight are metaphors commonly used in ancient religious literature to refer to spiritual insight or the lack of it. The writer builds on this generally accepted imagery in 1:18 when he informs his readers that they have had the eyes of their hearts enlightened. In the New Testament, "seeing" is a familiar metaphor for spiritual vision (Matthew 5:8; John 8:51; 1 Corinthians 13:12; Hebrews 2:9; 11:1), whereas

GALATIANS AND EPHESIANS

"blindness" is used to describe an inability or refusal to believe or have faith (Mark 4:11-12; 8:14-21, 22-26; 10:46-52; John 9; Acts 28:26-28). *Enlightened* refers to the revelation and knowledge given to Christians by God when they first accept the faith (see Ephesians 3:9). A similar concept is found in 2 Corinthians 4:6: *For it is the God who said, "Let light shine out of darkness," who has shown in our hearts to give the light of the knowledge of the glory of God in the face of Christ.*

For the meaning of the word *hope*, see the discussion of Galatians 5:5 above.

Thanks for What God Has Done (1:19-23)

In the last half of verse 18 and in verse 19, the writer once again piles up references to the riches available to those who know Christ and the great power of God in him (see the discussion of 1:9 above). The Greek word for *power* that he uses here is *dunamis*, and it is from this word that we get our English word *dynamite*. God's power in Christ is explosive, and it can accomplish all that God desires or plans (3:20). As Paul says in Romans 1:16, the gospel is *the power of God for salvation to everyone who has faith*. The same word is used throughout the New Testament to refer to Christ's healings and exorcisms, and is usually translated *miracle*. The writer says in Ephesians 3:7 that it is the power that made him a minister of the gospel and strengthens the inner, spiritual person (3:16). He mentions it in 1:19 because he wants to contrast the power of God to that possessed by the spiritual beings who are called *powers* in 3:10 and 6:12 (see also Colossians 2:15), those who oppose the lordship of Christ. They do not have any authority over Christians because of the surpassingly great power of God and the intensity of God's strength.

Ephesians 1:20-23 provides an example of the kernel of the Christian faith, as the author lists the essential things one must believe to be a Christian. It is possible that he is using the words of a Christian hymn here that was written in a simple way so that new converts could remember it easily. Similar passages are found in Acts 2:30-33, Romans 8:34, and Philippians. The essential elements of that faith include belief in Jesus' resurrection, his exaltation at God's right hand, and his authority over all spiritual powers.

Raised from the dead refers to the most fundamental element of the Christian faith, that Christ did not remain dead after his crucifixion, but after three days was raised up by God to new life. The Resurrection was preached as a keystone of faith (Acts 2:32; Romans 1:4), and in 1 Corinthians 15 Paul says that all belief is empty and pitiful without it (15:2, 3-8, 12-14, 19). In Romans 10:9 he puts it at the heart of the confession a new Christian must make. In Ephesians 2:1, 5-7, the writer indicates that God raised Jesus from the dead and will also raise those who believe in God to new life.

Put Him at the Right Hand (1:20)

Sit at his right hand in the heavenly places in verse 20 is a reference to the early Christian belief that after Jesus' death, God raised him up to a place of special prominence and power in heaven. In the Bible, *hand* is a symbol of power and authority (Exodus 13:3; 14:21; Deuteronomy 3:24; Job 19:21). God promises in Psalm 110:1 that only the messiah will have the ability to sit at the most important place of power, and that his enemies will be put at his feet. Christians believed that place to be given to Jesus (Mark 12:36; Acts 2:25; Hebrews 1:3). The same belief is still expressed today every time worshipers repeat the Apostles' Creed. It is this confidence in Christ's final power that is also expressed in the renowned words of Handel's *Messiah*, "King of kings, and Lord of lords. And he shall reign for ever and ever. Hallelujah!"

For *heavenly places* see the discussion of 1:3 above.

Gave Him Authority (1:21)

Verse 21 says that Jesus is far above all spiritual powers in authority and might. Since people in the ancient world often believed that there were several different levels of heaven with ascending orders of power, this writer says that Jesus is higher and stronger than any of them. Spiritual powers such as angels, rulers, principalities, powers, and authorities cannot intimidate or cause harm to Christians anymore because they have been defeated through Christ's death and resurrection. (See Romans 8:38-39; 1 Corinthians 15:24; Colossians 2:15.) They may have names which strike fear in human hearts, but Jesus' name, because it has been given to him by God, is above every name (Philippians 2:9-11), and it will remain so in this age and all through eternity (the age that is to come). (See Galatians 1:4 above.)

Put All Things Under His Feet (1:22)

Put all things under his feet in verse 22 is a reference to Psalm 8:6, where it is indicated that all the power of God will be given to those God designates. (See also Psalm 110:1.) Christians knew that this power had been transferred to Christ when he was placed on God's right hand. (See 1 Corinthians 15:27, Hebrews 2:5-8.)

Made Him Head of the Church (1:22-23)

In the second half of verse 22 and in verse 23, the writer summarizes the argument of 1:15-23 by indicating that God has made Jesus head over all things for the church. *Head* means that Christ is the highest spiritual power, not only on earth, but in the whole cosmos. No one or no thing has been given more power and authority than he has. As it says in 1:10, God *unites* or sums up all things in the Son. Once again, the closest parallels in the New Testament are found in Colossians. *He is the head of the body, the church; he is the beginning, the first-born from the dead, that in everything he might be pre-eminent* (Colossians 1:18). He is *the head of all rule and authority* (2:10). Christ is not only the head of all spiritual forces, but he is also the head of the church. The word *church* (*ekklesia* in Greek) appears prominently in Ephesians (3:10, 21; 5:23-32). It always refers to the universal church, not a congregation in a local area. In its most basic form, *ekklesia* means *assembly* or *gathering*, but the New Testament often refers to it as the *body of Christ*. *Body* was a common symbol in religious and medical literature at the time Ephesians was written, and the writer appears to be aware of the way it was used. In religious writings it was often said that the universe was like a huge human body with a god as its source or head. Inferior divinities such as authorities and powers were part of the body, but they were under the control of the head. Clearly, the writer is influenced by this kind of thinking since he is determined to demonstrate here that Christ is more powerful than all other spiritual beings. Another metaphor common in the ancient world was used by physicians who understood that muscles, limbs, and organs were controlled by the brain. Since the writer uses physiological terms in Ephesians 4:4 and 15-16 (see Colossians 2:19), he probably has this image in mind as well.

In Ephesians, the writer's use of the concept of the body is similar to that found in Romans 12:4-8, 1 Corinthians 12:12-27, and Colossians 1:18, which points to the unity of all things in Christ. In the Christian church, individual members must not think that they have power independent of Christ or that they are more important than other parts of the body. All members are prized and loved by him and are a part of him. Together they fill up his body as he fills all in all.

For the concept of fullness in Christ see the comments on Ephesians 1:10 above.

§ § § § § § §

The Message of Ephesians 1:15-23

§ In 1:15-23 the author of Ephesians thanks God for his readers' faith and prays that God will give them a spirit of wisdom and knowledge.

§ God has surpassing power, which is demonstrated by raising Jesus from the dead, giving him the highest seat of power in heaven, and making him head over all spiritual forces and over the church.

§ Since Christ is over all things and all living beings, everything is summed up and fulfilled in him.

§ § § § § § §

Ephesians 2:1-10

Introduction to These Verses

Chapter Two begins with another long sentence in Greek, this one extending from verse 1 all the way through verse 7, connected only with commas and colons.

Delivered From Death (2:1-3)

The writer begins with the words *And you he made alive.* *You* refers to his readers, the Gentiles to whom the letter is written (see 3:1). In verse 3 he will change over to *we*, indicating that he is speaking about himself and other Jews.

The contrast of being dead in trespasses and being made alive in Christ is not an unusual one in the New Testament (see John 5:24; Romans 11:15; 1 John 3:14). It indicates that the Christian is constantly faced with a choice of two ways that are diametrically opposed. One leads to spiritual and physical death, the other to spiritual life and resurrection with Christ. The same image is used in 5:14: *Awake, O sleeper, and arise from the dead, and Christ shall give you light.*

Possibly the writer has the sacrament of baptism in mind here, since the symbols of death and rising to new life are used in that connection in Colossians 2:12-14 and Romans 6:3-11. For the first Christians, being a follower of Christ made such a difference in their attitudes and actions that their former lives seemed dead by comparison to those that were now possible in Christ. As the apostle Paul says in Romans 6:11, *you also must consider yourselves dead to sin and alive to God in Christ Jesus.* The significance of Christ's resurrection is discussed in reference to 1:20 above.

For a discussion of the meaning of trespasses and sins see the comments on 1:7 above.

Verse 2 is very important in Ephesians because here the writer makes it clear that the two ways that beckon to the Christian involve more than a choice between a good ethical life or one that is bad. The choice places the believer either in a powerful heavenly realm that is good or one that is evil. He begins the verse with the words *in which you once walked.* To walk, as is pointed out in reference to Galatians 5:16, is a metaphor for the kind of life a person lives. It is used in Ephesians repeatedly (2:10; 5:2, 8, 15); 4:1 should be translated *I beg you to walk worthily of the calling.*

The Revised Standard Version translation, *following the course of this world,* seems to indicate that the two choices are between competing ethical, religious, or philosophical systems. The Greek words for *the course of this world* are *aion tou kosmou,* which may literally be translated *aeon of the cosmos.* Although the word *aion* can mean *age, this present time in history,* or *the evil time in which we live* (see 1:21; 2:7; 3:9; 1 Corinthians 1:20; 2:6-7; 3:18; Galatians 1:4, *present evil age*), it is more likely that in Ephesians 2:2 something quite different is intended. This word can also refer to gods or heavenly beings, and since the writer connects it here with the *prince of the power of the air* it no doubt means the *god of this age.* A close parallel is found in 2 Corinthians 4:4 where the same word is used, *the god of this world has blinded the minds of the unbelievers.* Thus the phrase is another term for the devil, and means *god of this age* or *world god.*

The prince of the power of the air is a descriptive expression that refers to the devil or Satan. The Greek word for *prince* could also designate kings, public officials, or authorities (*rulers*, Matthew 20:25; Luke 8:41; John 3:1), but it was often used in the ancient world to refer to angels, divine beings, or devils. In several passages, for example, it refers to Satan or Beelzebul as the *prince of demons* (Matthew 9:34; 12:24; Mark 3:22; Luke 11:15). He is the evil force in the universe who tries to destroy Christ and his kingdom. In John's Gospel he is referred to as *the ruler of this world* (John 12:31; 14:30; 16:11). For the writer of Ephesians, even though Satan has unimaginable power, Christians can choose to follow Jesus Christ instead. If they do, they will walk behind the one who is far above all rulers (1:21; 3:10), and the writer will equip them so they may overcome him (6:10-11).

Air refers to heaven or the heavenly places (see 1 Thessalonians 4:17 where the same word is used). *Sons of disobedience* are those who have disobeyed God and have chosen the prince of darkness as their Lord (see 5:6; Hebrews 4:6, 11). Disobedience is the main characteristic of those who are caught up in sin, in rebellion against God. (See Romans 11:30-32.)

In verse 3 the writer indicates that all human beings, whether they are Gentiles or Jews, are sinful and could succumb to the devil's tricks. In essence, he summarizes Paul's extended argument in Romans 1:18–3:18 where the apostle shows that all people are guilty of disobeying God, and need Christ to be made right with God.

Like the rest of mankind is very similar to Romans 3:9, which says that all people, both Jews and Greeks, *are under the power of sin.*

Children of wrath means that all people are liable to the righteous anger and judgment of God.

Made Alive Together in Christ (2:4-7)

In verses 4-6, the writer repeats what he has already said before in 1:5, 7, 18, 20, and 2:1 about the love of God in Christ, the richness of God's mercy, and the significance of the Resurrection. The parenthetical remark in verse 5 (*by grace you have been saved*), which is repeated in verse 8, is a concise summary of the kind of argument found throughout the writings of the apostle Paul, particulary in Galatians. (See the discussions of Galatians 1:6 and 2:16-21 above.) Grace is the free gift of God in Jesus Christ. Because of the forgiveness of sins that God gives believers in Christ, they no longer have to be trapped in sin or condemned to spiritual death. Instead, these believers hve been saved or ransomed by Christ's death on the cross, not by anything they do or do not do.

Most biblical scholars agree that verses 4-7 and verse 10 contain the words of a Christian hymn that the writer borrows from the liturgy of the early church. In Greek, these verses have a poetic style that sets them off from the rest of the section. They contain the essentials of faith that could be sung in worship or recited in a creed: *made us alive together with Christ—raised us up with him—made us sit with him in the heavenly places*. They contain the basis of the Easter hope and the fundamental promise of eternal life.

In the expression *the coming ages* (verse 7) the writer once again uses the Greek word *aion* (see the discussion of 2:2 above). The meaning in this verse is not certain, since the words could be translated to refer to eternity (*the ages to come*) or could mean *the divine rulers or demons that are coming at us*. Either interpretation is possible, since *aion* is used both ways in the letter. If it is used in the first sense, it means that Christ will be the ruler in all ages to come, even into eternity, forever and forever (see 3:21). If the second meaing is what the writer has in mind, then the reference is to the principalities and powers, the rulers and authorities, the devil and his cohorts who are constanty attacking Christ and his kingdom. Even though they are coming at Christ and those who follow him, they will not be victorious. His power in the heavenly places is absolute.

Saved by Faith (2:8-10)

In verse 8 the writer repeats the clause about God's grace from verse 5. (See the discussion there.) These verses summarize the fundamental insight that Jews are no longer put right with God by observing the Ten Commandments or the rules of the Jewish law. Salvation is achieved not by what people do but by what they believe. It is accomplished not through human actions, but by God's grace, God's free gifts in Christ, his death on the cross and his resurrection.

For *the danger of boasting* see the discussion of Galatians 6:4 above.

In verse 10 the writer plays on the word *work*. We are his workmanship and therefore made for good works. When he says that Christians are made by God in Christ, he refers once again (see 1:4-5) to the certainty that those who believe have been called from the foundation of the world and that Christ was present at that Creation. God, he implies, sees humanity as God's sculpture made in Christ. It is the new creation for the new age (2 Corinthians 5:17; Galatians 6:15). The *good works* for which humanity is created are not the *works* mentioned in verses 8 and 9, but the fruit of the Spirit that comes as a gift from God (see the discussions of Galatians 5:21-23 and Ephesians 4:4-17).

§ § § § § § §

The Message of Ephesians 2:1-10

§ In this section the author of Ephesians reminds his readers of the danger they are in from sins and trespasses and from the power of the devil. When people rebel against God and become children of disobedience they face the possibility of spiritual death. They also have to be careful not to follow the devil, who is known as the world god and the *prince of the power of the air*.

§ Although all human beings, whether they are Gentiles or Jews, are sinful by nature and fall under God's judgment, in Christ Jesus they have been forgiven for their sins, they have been given new spiritual life, and they have been delivered from the power of the devil and all the spiritual beings who are in allegiance with him.

§ Being put right with God means that Christians are raised up with Christ, made to sit with him on the right hand of power, and given the free gift of forgiveness by God. Those who believe in Christ are his creation and they are made to do good works, to walk in the fruit of the Spirit.

§ § § § § § §

Ephesians 2:11-22

Introduction to These Verses

In this section the author of Ephesians demonstrates how the ancient distinction between Jews and Gentiles has been demolished by Jesus Christ.

You Were Once Refugees of Faith (2:11-12)

In verse 11, the writer addresses his Gentile readers directly once more. He has referred to them as *you* before (1:13, 16, 17; 2:1) and calls them *you Gentiles* here (see 3:1). *Gentiles* is a name that the Jews gave to those who were not believers in the Jewish faith, those who did not subscribe to the principles of the law. The writer points out that they were also called *the uncircumcision* by the Jews, meaning that they were pagans who did not show themselves to be part of God's covenant by having their foreskins surgically removed. See the discussion in reference to Galatians 2:3-10 above. The Jews, on the other hand, referred to themselves as *the circumcision*, a term of superiority from their point of view. The writer indicates that he does not think that circumcision should be a matter of pride when he refers to it as something *which is made in the flesh by hands*. Circumcision is a manufactured symbol and does not necessarily imply spiritual maturity since it may or may not come from God. Colossians 2:11 makes a similar point when it says that true spiritual strength comes only from spiritual circumcision in Christ: *In him also you were circumcised with a circumcision made without hands, by putting off the body in the flesh in the circumcision of Christ.* (See also Romans 2:28-29.)

When the writer lists the spiritual characteristics of the Gentiles, he wants to remind them how much they need Jesus Christ. They were *separated from Christ, alienated from the commonwealth of Israel, strangers to the covenants of promise, wihout hope* and *without God in the world*. These were all spiritual gifts which the Jews could have had if they had remained faithful to God (see Paul's emotional recollection in Romans 9:4-5). But their loss is the Gentiles' gain. Now the covenant, the commonwealth, and the promise belong to all people.

Separated from Christ means that since they had no connection with Israel's Scripture, law, or prophets, they did not know about the coming messiah who was promised to the Jews. It also means that as Gentiles they did not believe in Christ and therefore were not aware of his power or love. For a Christian, to be separated from Christ is almost the definition of Hell since he is, as the writer says, all in all.

Alienated from the commonwealth of Israel indicates that the Gentiles were never part of the people of God, never part of that great fellowship that enabled Jews to know that they were God's children no matter where they were in the world. Here the writer uses a political term which refers to aliens or outsiders who are not citizens of a city (see 2:19). Those who do not have citizenship are always under suspicion and do not have the rights given to natives.

Having no hope refers to the condition of those who do not believe in Christ. Without Christ, they have no hope of being put right with God; they cannot look forward to life after death (see 1 Thessalonians 4:13). In Christ, God has become the God of hope to those who once had no hope at all (Romans 15:13). For a more complete discussion of the New Testament idea of hope, see the comments above on Galatians 5:5.

In the phrase *without God in the world*, the writer uses the Greek word *atheos*. This is the same word from which we derive the English word *atheist*. It refers to the Jewish belief that even though Gentiles believed in gods and goddesses whom they represented in idols, these so-called divine beings did not really exist at all. Thus those who worshiped them were atheists, believers in "no gods." *Without God* also refers to the concept that God is separated from those who refuse to believe (see Romans 1:28).

Those Far Away Are Brought Near (2:13)

The words *but now in Christ Jesus* form a key phrase for the writer as he turns from that which the Gentiles lacked to what they now have in Jesus Christ. Jesus is the key to new life, new citizenship, and a new relationship to God. Everything is changed *in Christ* and all old animosities and barriers between God and humanity and between different races and nations are broken down and demolished forever. Christ has brought peace.

Far off . . . brought near is probably an allusion to the prophetic word in Isaiah 57:19, *Peace, peace, to the far and the near, says the* Lord, *and I will heal him.* The same Scripture is referred to in Ephesians 2:17 below. Similar ideas are found elsewhere in the Old Testament where God promises that those who were called *not his people* before could become *his people* now (Hosea 1:9-10; 2:23; Romans 9:25-26; 1 Peter 2:10).

The phrase *in the blood of Christ* is a reference to the fact that the reconciliation of the Gentiles was brought about by Christ's death on the cross. The writer's understanding is clearly a sacrificial one here. Just as cattle and sheep had to be sacrificed at the altar in order for the Jews to draw close to God (see Exodus 24:4-8), Christians are put right with God by the blood of Christ shed on the cross. (See Colossians 1:20-22; Hebrews 10:19-22; 1 John 1:7.)

The Wall of Hostility Is Broken Down (2:14-18)

In verses 14-18 the writer inserts another Christian hymn borrowed from the worship services of the early church. Probably it is one that is well-known to his Gentile readers and strikes a responsive chord with them. He has used hymns before in Ephesians to remind them of the essential elements of their faith (see the discussions of 1:2-23 and 2:4-7 above), and the one he uses here is very similar to that quoted in Colossians 1:21-22.

The writer indicates in verse 14 that the division and hostility that have always existed between the Jews and the Gentiles throughout history have now been abolished in Jesus Christ because *he is our peace*. Peace, as verse 13 points out, is brought about by the reconciling love of Christ's blood shed on the cross, which makes all people one. Since, as Paul says in Romans 1 and 2, all human beings stand before God as sinners and without excuse, they all need Jesus to be put right with God whether they are Gentiles or Jews. As he says in Galatians 3:28, all distinctions are broken down in Christ, since all who believe in him *put on Christ* and are *in him*. A similar image is used in Romans 5:6-11 where the apostle indicates that those who were once enemies with God and with each other are brought together or reconciled. They are able to live peacefully together through the death and resurrection of Jesus. For a discussion of the meaning of *peace* see Galatians 1:3 above.

In the writer's view Gentiles and Jews are enabled to be at peace because they are no longer two separate peoples pulling and tugging at each other, but are now like one person with two separate but joined parts. Just as kingdoms and houses cannot be divided if they are to survive (Mark 3:24-25), so a body cannot function if the individual parts which make it up are at war with each other. The Christian church is now composed of many different groups of people who compose Christ's one body. The eye cannot say to the ear that it does not need to hear, and the ear cannot say to the leg that it does not need to walk (1 Corinthians 12:12-25). The body functions as one living organism to meet the goals and needs of the head. The church in Christ represents the new humanity which God envisions for all people everywhere. The same point is made in verses 15-16 below. For further comments on the *one body* see the discussion of Ephesians 1:22-23 and 4:4, 11-13.

When the writer says that Christ has *broken down the dividing wall of hostility* he uses graphic language to draw a picture of the difference Christ makes in the lives of those who were once at war with one another spiritually. The Greek word for *dividing wall* is *phragmos* and in its most basic sense refers to a fence, a railing, or a hedge used for protection (Isaiah 5:5; Matthew 21:33).

The writer may have several different ideas in mind here. There was a dividing wall in the Jerusalem Temple that separated the Outer Court of the Gentiles, which anyone could enter, from the rest of the Temple, which was only open to Jews. Gentiles who passed beyond that wall did so under penalty of death. It may be that the writer is thinking here of that dividing wall finally being broken down so that all people of the world could worship God together in the same place in peace. By the time Ephesians was written, the Temple was literally in ruins, since Jerusalem had been destroyed in A.D. 70 by the Romans. The shell of the Temple that remained could symbolize to Christians that God would not allow the former hostility between Gentiles and Jews to stand. For those two peoples, historically divided so long, it would have been a symbol as powerful as the breaking down of the Berlin Wall and the Iron Curtain between East and West Germany would be today.

A second meaning that the writer may have given to the word *wall* was that it stood for the Jewish law and the commandments and ordinances (2:15). Since rabbis later referred to the law as a "fence" erected by God to keep the Jews from Gentile contamination, it may be that the writer is reminding his readers that the demands of the law are also broken down in Christ (see 2:8 above). As he says in verse 15, Christ became peace by *abolishing in his flesh the law of commandments and ordinances*.

A third concept that the picture of the wall might bring to the minds of the readers of Ephesians is that of the separation created between God and humanity by sin. Spiritual divisions exist not only between different peoples, but also between God and individuals. The Bible repeatedly warns that rebellion against God will cause God to withdraw from the people. As Isaiah 59:2 says, *. . . your iniquities have made a separation between you and your God, and your sins have hid his face from you so that he does not hear*. Paul uses an even stronger metaphor in Romans where he says that God gives up to sin those who are determined to be ruled by it (1:24, 26). Human beings can be so disloyal to God that they can actually become God's enemies (Romans 5:10). The dividing wall, then, is not only a horizontal one between different groups of people, but is a vertical one between humanity and the Creator. Thus in verse 16 the writer rejoices that both elements are reconciled in Christ by the vertical and horizontal beams of the cross, thereby bringing *hostility* to an end.

In verse 16 the writer uses the verb *reconcile* to describe Christ's action of destroying spiritual hostility. *Reconcile* means to improve or restore a relationship between persons or groups who were at one time at war with each other. The same word is used in Colossians 1:21-22: *And you, who once were estranged and hostile in mind, doing evil deeds, he* [Christ] *has now reconciled in his body of flesh by his death*. The noun *reconciliation* is used similarly in the New Testament to indicate the way in which Christ brings peace with God (Romans 5:11; 11:15; 2 Corinthians 5:19).

For *access* in verse 18 see the discussion of 3:12 below.

You Are Now Fellow Citizens (2:19)

In verse 19 the writer changes symbols from the dividing wall of hostility to the mixed metaphors of the city of Christ, the household of God, and the living temple.

Here he uses an image similar to the one employed in verse 12. At one time the distinction was drawn so severely between Jews and Gentiles that the Gentiles must have felt as though they were aliens and refugees in the city of God. Although the Jews were commanded to treat *strangers and sojourners* with special care (Deuteronomy 10:18-19; 27:19; Job 31:32), outsiders were governed by different laws (Leviticus 24:22) and were probably generally regarded with suspicion. In Greek and Roman cities citizenship was usually dependent on birth rather than residence, and foreigners could gain it only by special decree. In some cities it was possible to be given a second-class status, which meant that a person had all the individual rights of citizenship but could not vote or hold office. Citizenship was a very valuable commodity in the Roman Empire, and without it one might not have equal protection under the law (see Acts 22:22-29). In Ephesians 2:19 the writer makes it clear that such distinctions do not exist in the church of Jesus Christ. The Gentiles are now *fellow citizens* with the *saints* (those set apart or called by God to be in the church, 1:1) and *members of the household of God.*

Household of God refers to the fact that, in Christ, all Christians, whether Gentiles or Jews, are members of one family and have the same rights and privileges. All believers are children of the same God and are truly God's sons and daughters. The writer may also be thinking of the fact here that the early Christians often did not have sanctuaries and met regularly in private homes (see the comments on Galatians 6:10 above).

Recent research demonstrates that the household was a basic unit in the society of the ancient world in Greece and Rome. Extended families (fathers, mothers, grandparents, children, and slaves) functioned as a unit and the members were bound together by strict codes of honor and duty. The household rules in Ephesians 5:21–6:9 are a variation of the kind of expectations that most people understood. In Roman society, for example, people were connected through these codes not so much by feelings of love as by hierarchical order. Individuals were to obey the Emperor, the nation, and the head of the house (usually the father), in that order (see Romans 13:1; 1 Peter 2:13-14, 17). In some circles it was believed that if order in the family could be preserved, then all larger institutions could be expected to survive. If a father could not control his own house, on the other hand, how could he, or anyone else, be expected to govern a city or a nation (or a church—see 1 Timothy 3:4-5). The author of Ephesians builds on this kind of understanding when he tells Christians that their household is built on a somewhat different order. Christians do not owe primary honor to the Emperor, but to Jesus Christ. He is the head of their house (1:22; 5:22-24), and Gentiles and Jews both are children in it.

The Foundation and Cornerstone (2:20)

The writer continues with the metaphor of the house and the church. The church of Jesus Christ is God's new house *built upon the foundation of the apostles and the prophets*. As noted in the Introduction, this verse is an indication that Ephesians probably was not written by the apostle Paul. The writer indicates here that Jesus is the keystone of the church (as *cornerstone* should correctly be translated), but that the apostles and prophets (Christian prophets—see 1 Corinthians 12:10) are the *foundation*. The apostle Paul, however, thinks of Jesus Christ alone as the foundation and cornerstone in 1 Corinthians 3:11. It is extremely unlikely, furthermore, that he would refer to the apostles as the building blocks of the church as if he were not among them himself. As he demonstrates repeatedly in Galatians, his apostleship is a critical part of the proof of his authority.

The image of Jesus as the cornerstone of the church is a common one in the New Testament (Matthew 21:42; Acts 4:11; 1 Peter 2:4-8), and Ephesians reflects a time in the life of the church when Christians were trying to determine who should have power in the church. The author indicates here that leaders have to be in line with the original founders of the church who had the titles of prophets and apostles.

The Living House (2:21-22)

Verses 21-22 complete the comparison of the house and the church by picturing the church as a building that is a living being, an organism in which God lives. Here he builds on the Old Testament idea that the place in which God is worshiped is the house in which God dwells (2 Chronicles 5:14; Psalm 122:1). He also uses a physiological model: The house of God is like a human body, intricately put together with tissue, bones, and joints (see 4:15-16). For him the church is no longer a dwelling place, a building, or a steeple. The church is a living body; it is people (see 1 Peter 2:5; 4:17).

Temple in verse 21 refers to the inner sanctuary that formed the most revered part of the Jerusalem Temple. The writer tells his readers that what was once the Holy of Holies, or the inner sanctum of God, is replaced by the Christian church, the place where God now dwells. As Paul says in 1 Corinthians, *You are . . . God's building* (3:9); *. . . God's temple is holy, and that temple you are* (3:17).

§ § § § § § §

The Message of Ephesians 2:11-22

§ The separation caused by circumcision, the sign of the Old Testament covenant, is no longer valid. There is no longer circumcision and uncircumcision.

§ Gentiles also are no longer alienated from God as they were at one time. They are not aliens and refugees in God's city anymore, but are now full citizens with equal rights and privileges.

§ Jesus Christ has broken down the wall between Jews and Gentiles which was symbolized by the wall that kept Gentiles out of the Jerusalem Temple. He has broken down the fence which the law put around the Jews. He has destroyed the hostility that existed between God and humanity. Through his blood, his sacrifice on the cross, Christ has brought peace.

§ Gentiles now co-exist as members of one family, brothers and sisters in one household of God. Together they make up a living house which is where God may dwell and truly be worshiped.

§ § § § § § §

Ephesians 3:1-13

Introduction to These Verses

In this section the author of Ephesians attempts to link his letter with the life of the apostle Paul and repeats several themes which have already been introduced in the first two chapters. In verses 14-21 he also finishes the uncompleted prayer begun in 1:16-17. Chapter 4 begins a second major part of the letter.

A Steward of the Mystery (3:1-3)

The writer refers to the fact that he is a prisoner for Christ Jesus. A similar description is repeated in 4:1. He mentions this to his Gentile readers to remind them that the apostle's arrest and imprisonment arose directly out of his mission to them and out of his desire to bring offerings from Gentile Christians to the impoverished believers in Jerusalem (Acts 17–28). Paul literally was a prisoner on several different occasions (Acts 28:17-31; Philippians 1:12-18; Colossians 4:18).

Assuming that you have heard is not the kind of language that would be expected from someone who knew the Ephesians as well as the apostle Paul did (Acts 18:19-21; 19:1-20; 20:17-38). It indicates that someone other than Paul probably wrote the letter.

The concept of the stewardship of God's grace is an important one in this writer's understanding of the message of Christ. The word *stewardship* is *oikonomos* in Greek. It comes from the Greek word for house (*oikos*) and literally means *law of the house*. As the discussion of

2:11-22 demonstrates, the idea of the "house" is a key one in Ephesians. In its most basic sense *stewardship* means *management, direction, plan,* and *oikonomos* is used in 1:10 to describe God's plan for the fullness of time. The stewardship of God's grace describes God's administration or plan of salvation as it is worked out in Jesus Christ for those in the house of faith. God's strategy is to bring people into a right relationship. Stewardship defines God's flowchart of redemption. A steward is a "manager" (see Luke 12:42; 16:1-4; 1 Corinthians 4:1-2; in Romans 16:23 the word describes a city treasurer). In the church a steward is a servant of Christ given authority to manage God's mysteries (1 Corinthians 4:1); he or she must be blameless in conduct (Titus 1:7) and a manager of *God's varied grace* (1 Peter 4:10).

Mystery and revelation have already been discussed above (1:9; 1:17-18). The mystery for this writer is the inclusion of the Gentiles within God's great plan of salvation (3:6).

As I have written briefly refers to what has already been said in Ephesians 1–2, the other letters this writer has written, earlier letters of the apostle Paul, or possibly even similar words found in Colossians 1:25-28.

The Message Is Now Revealed (3:4-6)

The author claims in this section that the revelation of the mystery of God is something that has taken place only recently. It has not been revealed to people in other generations (the Jews, or pagans who believed in idols), but is now made known to the holy apostles and the prophets. Thus he denies once again that the truth of God has been revealed through the Jewish law (see 2:11-13) or through the Gnostic religion (see the Introduction). *Prophets* probably does not refer to the Old Testament prophets who only had a partial vision of the coming messiah, but to Christian prophets (1 Corinthians 12:29) who have been fully informed by the Spirit.

Not made known in verse 5 indicates the writer's concern about the matter of knowledge, who has it and where it comes from (see the Introduction). The mystery of God has been reserved; it was not made known until it was time for God's plan of stewardship to be completed (see Mark 1:15; 4:11). That is why it is a mystery; it is a secret until God chooses to make it known. (See Romans 16:25-27.)

The words *holy apostles* are unusual ones and another indication that Paul may not have written the letter. By writing this way the writer makes it clear that the apostles composed a group of people who must be revered and that he was not among them himself.

By the Spirit (verse 5) points to the belief in the early church that God's plan for salvation was not fully made known until the period after Jesus' resurrection and ascension (Acts 2). Apostles and prophets were given their management of the gospel as direct gifts from God's Holy Spirit (Ephesians 4:11; 1 Corinthians 12:29). The Spirit is a Spirit of revelation, one who uncovers the truth (Ephesians 1:17).

Verse 6 refers back to the concept of the one body in Christ mentioned in 1:23 and 2:14-16. In this verse the writer uses three nouns which begin with the Greek preposition *sun*, which means *with* or *in*. Christians are involved together in the body of Christ as heirs with each other (*joint heirs*; see 1 Peter 3:7), members with each other (*members in the same body*), and sharers of the promise with each other (*partakers*). They are all in it together, with each other, and in Christ (*sun Christ*; see the discussion in 1:1 above).

The Least of the Apostles (3:7-13)

The word *minister* in verse 7 is *diakonos* in Greek and literally means *servant*. It is similar to Paul's description of himself in Galatians 1:10 as a slave of Christ. The word *servant* is the same one used in Acts 6:1-6 to describe the first deacons in the church, those selected by the Spirit to make up the caring arm of the community of faith. See Philippians 1:1; Colossians 1:7; and 1 Thessalonians 3:2 where other Christians are called servants.

Many of the words and expressions used in this section have appeared already in Ephesians: for *power* see 1:19; *riches*, 1:7, 18; *plan, stewardship*, 3:2; *creator of all things*, 1:4; *principalities, heavenly places*, Introduction, 1:3, 20, 21-23; *eternal purpose*, 1:9-10; *glory*, 1:14, 17.

Hidden for the ages in God is probably a mistranslation of the Greek word *aion*. See the discussion of 2:2 above. A correct translation might be *hidden from the aion*, that is, hidden from the divine beings who make up one level of the heavens. The same idea is found in 3:10. The truth of God's plan of salvation was even hidden from spiritual powers, but now that Christ has been raised it can be revealed by God to them too.

Access is a word that Paul borrows from life in royal palaces. *Having access* refers to the right to appear before a king or a judge. In the ancient world the "accessor" or chamberlain was the one who decided who could see the official in power. The writer says in verses 12 and 13 that Christ is the *accessor* who gives believers the right even to approach God.

§ § § § § § §

The Message of Ephesians 3:1-13

§ The author of Ephesians ties his letter in with the life of the apostle Paul and his imprisonment.

§ The author has been given the mystery of God. It was made known to him by the stewardship of grace. Stewardship refers to God's plan or flow chart of salvation. The mystery is that God admitted the Gentiles into the family of faith.

§ God's uncovering of the mystery has been given only recently. It was not given to the Jews in the past or to those who believed in pagan religions, but only to Christian apostles and prophets. It was even hidden from divine beings who live in the heavens, but now they also know the truth through Christ. Jesus is the one who allows all living creatures to know God and have access to God.

§ § § § § § §

Ephesians 3:14-21

Introduction to These Verses

Ephesians 3:14-21 is one of the most beautiful passages in the whole Bible, reaching beyond words to express how wonderful it is to have the Holy Spirit in the inner person of faith. When Christians have Christ in them and are enlivened and motivated by his love, they can only break out in praise about the incomprehensible dimensions of all that God gives.

Empowered Internally by the Spirit (3:14-16)

Bow my knees expresses an attitude of prayer and wonder. The writer has already said in 3:7 that he is a *servant*, so humility before God is the proper attitude of faith. Although Jews usually stood when they prayed, the Bible often mentions bending the knees or "falling" on one's face as well (1 Kings 8:54; Daniel 6:10; Mark 14:35; Acts 7:60; 21:5). Possibly he mentions kneeling here because it was a customary way of praying for Gentiles.

The expression *every family* makes a play on words because in Greek the word for *father* (verse 14) and the word for *family* (verse 15) are very similar. All those who are in groups called *families* (*patria*) are named after the Father (*pater*). Verse 15 indicates God's lordship over all beings in this world and out of it. A family includes those related by blood and whole nations (Acts 3:25). It was also a word used in Jewish literature to describe angels. For the writer it is already clear that all beings, earthly or heavenly, are under the control of God.

In verse 16 reference is made to the *inner man* who is strengthened through God's Spirit. Although some scholars think that the inner man is Jesus Christ who is "in" the Christian (verse 17), the parallel expressions in Romans 7:22 and 2 Corinthians 4:16 indicate that the writer is thinking about the inner spiritual nature of the individual Christian. Possibly it is another expression for the human heart, the interior part of each person which must be committed to God for real spiritual transformation to take place. If, as Paul says in Galatians 2:20, Christ lives in the Christian, then it is at that place where spiritual enrichment and strengthening occur. Clearly it is not in the physical nature, which can easily be tempted and led astray (Galatians 5:16-17). For *Spirit* see the discussion of Galatians 3:5 above.

The Dimensions of Faith (3:17-19)

For the concept of Christ dwelling in the inner Christian and being "in Christ" see the discussion of Galatians 2:20 above. *Dwell* comes from the same root word in Greek as house. See the discussion of Ephesians 2:11-22 above. For the writer Christians are part of the same household of faith and Christ lives in that spiritual home. *Rooted and grounded* continues the same metaphor and refers to the foundation of a house. Christians live in a house with Christ as the cornerstone (2:20).

The beautiful passage in verse 18 (*the breadth and length and height and depth*) refers to the unlimited dimensions of the power of faith and the unimaginable power of God. Although it is difficult to know exactly what the writer has in mind here, similar language is found in many ancient religions. Job 11:8-9, for example, says that the wisdom of God is *deeper than Sheol . . . longer than the earth, and broader than the sea*. An ancient Greek papyrus refers to a god as the holy light, holy beam, breadth, depth, length, and height. It is also possible that the writer is once again responding to Gnostic ideas about the many different levels of reality on earth and in the heavens. He may be reiterating the fact that God is beyond anything that the human mind can imagine (see Romans 11:33-36). Perhaps verse 18 is merely a poetic way to say again that the fullness of the universe is in God who is all in all (Ephesians 1:23).

Verse 19 indicates that all of this is so amazing and so wonderful that it even surpasses knowledge. Even though some of his opponents may think that they have divine *gnosis* (see the Introduction, 1:17), they really do not know much when it comes to the power of the God who rules the universe. The key word, in fact, is not knowledge at all, but it is love, particularly the love of Christ (verses 17, 19; see 1:6 above).

A Benediction (3:20-21)

As is often the case in the Bible, when writers have said all that can be said and even more than that, there is nothing left to do but praise God (Romans 9:5; 11:36; Galatians 1:5; 1 Timothy 1:17; 2 Timothy 4:18). Thus the writer piles up words he has used before to express the tremendous feelings of love and admiration he has for God who has given him so much in Christ. *Amen* means *be it so* and is a fitting word with which to end this doxology (see Galatians 1:5 above) and to close the first section of the letter.

§ § § § § § §

The Message of Ephesians 3:14-21

§ In this section Ephesian's author expresses his praise for the immeasurable power and love of God in Christ. Because God cannot be fully known, the writer can only get on his knees and express gratitude to the one who showers believers with so much love.

§ God gives and gives to those who follow Christ. God strengthens the heart and empowers the inner person where spiritual nurturing takes place, so that God may be more fully understood.

§ The writer expresses gratitude for all of God's wonderful gifts, and prepares to move on to the second half of the letter.

§ § § § § § §

Ephesians 4

Introduction to This Chapter

In Chapter 4 the author of Ephesians begins the second major section of the letter. This part consists almost entirely of ethical advice, or what is often called exhortation. It was common for ancient writers, Christian and non-Christian, to give this kind of advice to their readers. Examples can be found in every New Testament letter, although they usually are not as long as here.

Lead a Worthy Life (4:1-3)

For discussion of the word *prisoner* see 3:1 above. *Lead a life* could literally be translated *walk*. See the discussion of 2:1 above. For *called* see 1:8. In the first verse the writer asks his readers to live as members of the Christian family and to be worthy of the name of Christ they bear as Christians.

He begins his advice by calling attention to four fruits of the Spirit which the believer can and should experience in daily life. See the discussion of meekness and patience in Galatians 5:22-23. *Forbearing one another in love* literally means *putting up with one another*. Sometimes life in the Christian church is not easy, and believers have to tolerate one another and overlook annoying faults. (See Mark 9:19; Acts 18:14; 2 Corinthians 11:1; Colossians 3:13.) In all cases love is the key component, the best gift of the Spirit and the most important fruit (see the discussion of Galatians 5:14, 22).

For *in one Spirit* see Galatians 3:28; 1 Corinthians 12:13; for *peace* see Ephesians 2:14 and Galatians 1:3.

The Oneness of Faith (4:4-6)

In verse 4 the writer returns to subjects he has introduced earlier in the letter, the one Holy Spirit (1:13-14), the one body of Christ (1:22-23; 2:15-16), hope, and calling (1:18). Similar passages are found in Romans 12:4-8; 1 Corinthians 8:6; 12:4-6.

The beautiful expression of the Christian faith found in verses 5-6, *one Lord, one faith, one baptism, one God and Father of us all*, may be an early example of a Christian creed which later developed into the well-known Nicean Creed and the Apostles' Creed. Unity exists for Christians because of a common faith, a common beginning in that faith (baptism), and the organic oneness of the church, which is the body of Christ Jesus. (See Romans 6:3; 1 Corinthians 12:13; Galatians 3:27.) The unity of faith is found in the solidarity of God as well, one God in three parts: the Father, the Lord Jesus, and the Spirit present in baptism. For a discussion of the words *above all* and *in all* see the Introduction and 1:23.

The Gifts of the Spirit (4:7-14)

Verses 7-14 are very similar to Romans 12:3-8 and 1 Corinthians 12:7-10, where the apostle Paul discusses the gifts of the Holy Spirit given to individual members of the body of Christ. They are given freely by the Spirit (grace) and by the measure (in Greek, *metron*) of Christ. Each person receives these gifts according to his or her God-given abilities and the needs of the church. *Measure* (verse 13) indicates that each Christian is not given every gift of the Spirit, that God imposes limits on what each receives. Thus Christians need to be united and work together for the body to have all the parts it needs (verses 16-17 below; 1 Corinthians 12:4-7).

The writer illustrates his understanding of the unity of

the church with a quotation of Psalm 68:18. Apparently this verse, even though its connection with the gifts of the Spirit seems somewhat obscure to modern readers, was considered to be a good prooftext for early Christians since it is similarly quoted in Romans 10:6-7. In Psalm 68 it is used as a victory song, showing God's power over all enemies. (See Proverbs 30:4.) The text here is not based on the original Hebrew from the Old Testament, but on an Aramaic version familiar to rabbis and early Christians.

The writer provides what he considers to be an explanation of Psalm 68:18 in verses 9 and 10. This was a common practice among rabbis, and in the Dead Sea Scrolls it was called a *pesher (interpretation)*. Its application to the matters being discussed in Ephesians is that it demonstrates that Jesus is Lord of all areas of existence, whether in heaven (ascended) or in Hell (descended) (see John 3:13). For this writer, *He led a host of captives* refers to the principalities and powers mentioned in 1:21 and 3:10 which have been defeated in spiritual battle by Jesus. The picture he provides here is one of Jesus as the conquering general returning from the war, publicly displaying the prisoners of war in a parade and distributing to his people the spoils of that war. (See Colossians 2:15.) In the case of the church, Christ's victory over the hostile spirits means that Jesus can give his people the gifts of the Holy Spirit.

In verse 11 the writer gives only four examples of gifts given to Christians to enable them to fill necessary offices in the church. Romans 12:6-8 and 1 Corinthians 12:28-30 provide more complete lists. He puts apostles first as that office which was first established to organize the church (see 1 Corinthians 12:28, *God has appointed in the church first apostles*). For the background of apostleship see Galatians 1:1 above. For *prophets* see Ephesians 2:20; 3:5.

Evangelists are called by God to preach the gospel (*good news*) of Jesus Christ (see Acts 21:8; 2 Timothy 4:5). See the discussion of *gospel* in Galatians 1:6 above.

The basic meaning of the word *pastors* is *shepherds of the flock*. The Scriptures often refer to those who care for God's people as God's shepherds. Just as God (or Jesus) is the good shepherd (Psalm 23; Mark 6:34; John 10:1-8; Hebrews 13:20), so the Christian pastor is expected to love the flock and work hard to protect it (Ezekiel 34; John 21:16; Acts 20:28).

Christian teachers are mentioned in Romans 2:20; 1 Timothy 2:7; 2 Timothy 4:3.

To equip the saints is a military image that the writer uses to convey the knowledge that God has given gifts of the Spirit to members of the church to prepare them for spiritual battle (see 6:10-20). The church is always to be on military alert against the strategies of evil.

For building up the body of Christ is a repetition of the symbol of the church as the living house of God already used in 2:19-22.

In verses 14-15 the writer shifts metaphors from the house to that of the mature Christian who is "grown up" in Christ. Christian maturity means that the believer is no longer a spiritual child, one who is still being nurtured on elementary Christian teaching (1 Corinthians 3:1-2; Hebrews 5:12-14; 1 Peter 2:2).

The Christian, if he or she is truly "in Christ", if he or she is really part of the body of Christ, is part of the fullness of Christ and shares the unity of the faith and the knowledge of the Son of God. Maturity is necessary to distinguish truth from falsehood and to prevent being carried about like a ship without a rudder by every puff of doctrine.

The Scriptures warn that false teachings and heresies will always tempt those who are not spiritually grown up (Acts 20:30; 2 Corinthians 11:3-4; 2 Thessalonians 2:9-12; 1 John 4:6). Human enemies of the gospel will use tricks and clever strategies (*cunning, deceitful wiles*, see 6:11). That is why the believer needs spiritual equipment to fight the constant onslaught on faith.

The Way a Body Should Function (4:15-16)

The writer returns in verses 15-16 to the image of the one body in Christ. The model is a physiological one here, the church being like a human body which functions in harmony by the proper working of nerves, muscles, ligaments, and bones, all parts being directed by the brain, the head of the body. All parts grow together, so that the body is in perfect proportion. A similar idea is expressed in Colossians 2:19, where it is said that *the whole body, nourished and knit together through its joints and ligaments, grows with a growth that is from God.* According to Ephesians 4:15, the element that unites the body is the self-giving love given by God in Christ to believers. This same love is given in turn by church members to one another.

Put on the New Nature (4:17–5:20)

The author introduces practical examples of how Christians should act and should not act by elaborating on what has already been said in 2:11-22: The Gentiles were once alienated from God by their pagan unbelief, but now that they have put on Christ they are fully part of his body. Since they are in Christ and he is in them they must act like Christ and represent him.

Do Not Live as the Gentiles Do (4:17-19)

The writer has already indicated that the Gentiles were alienated from God before they knew Christ (2:11-12; also see Romans 1:18-31, especially verse 21). *Futility of their minds* (4:17) probably refers to the worship of idols (see Acts 14:11-15; 1 Thessalonians 1:9-10).

For *darkened in their understanding* and *hardness of heart* (4:18) as symbols of spiritual blindness, see the discussion of 1:18 above. Hardness of heart refers to a calcified spiritual attitude (see verse 19, *callous*) which does not see because it refuses to see (Mark 3:5; 4:10-12; 8:11-18; 2 Corinthians 3:14).

He mentions *licentiousness* in verse 19 as a result of estrangement from God, because sexual immorality was considered to be a particular problem for Gentiles. See the discussion of Galatians 5:19 above. Also see 1 Peter 4:3; 2 Peter 2:2; Jude 4.

Be Renewed in the Spirit (4:20-24)

Changing from the negative images of alienation and spiritual blindness that once characterized the Gentiles, the author encourages his readers to live the new life in Christ by being so close to Christ that they actually put him on. This baptismal metaphor is a familar one to describe how close believers can be to their Lord—he is as near to them as their own clothing. He makes new men and women out of them (*new nature*, 4:24). See the detailed discussions in Galatians 3:27; 6:15 above.

In order for this new attitude to be dominant and for new behavior to take place, Christians need to be renewed in their inner spirits (4:23, *be renewed in the spirits of your minds*). Renewal is an action of God's Holy Spirit that allows believers to stop being worried by the external standards of the world (Romans 12:2) and to become more and more in tune with what God wants in Christ (Psalm 51:10; Romans 6:4; 2 Corinthians 4:16).

Tell the Truth (4:25)

The writer gives a long list of examples of what it means to think and act like one who has been renewed by the Holy Spirit, like one who is part of the body of Christ. In verse 25 he first reinforces the Old Testament commandment against lying (Exodus 20:16; Zechariah 8:16). Lying is wrong not only because God says so. It is a violation of the solidarity of the one body of Christ (Colossians 3:9-10), and it does not show the love toward one's neighbor that Jesus demands (Galatians 5:14). Christians tell the truth because Jesus himself is the truth (Ephesians 4:21; John 14:6).

Do Not Remain Angry (4:26-27)

The writer shares an insight here that is based on human psychology. It is not healthy to swallow anger and grievances. Anger is a normal response to the frustrations of life and it must be expressed. But it is also bad to let anger continue unchecked. (See Psalm 4:4.) Christians must resolve to settle differences with their neighbors within twenty-four hours to avoid the development of poisonous relationships that will harm the body of Christ. By being angry for extended periods, hostility to God and to neighbors increases and evil is given a chance to dominate. The Christian, in the author's view, must always be wary of the devil's desire to defeat the people of faith. (See Ephesians 6:11; 2 Corinthians 2:11.) Generally speaking, anger and hostility are characteristics that must be avoided in the church (Ephesians 4:31).

Thieves Must Reform (4:28)

Stealing is a major violation of God's moral code (Exodus 20:15; 22:1-3; Matthew 19:18) and cannot be permitted in the church. Thieves must be reformed and renewed by the Spirit and begin to do honest work again. They must become good stewards of their own resources so that instead of being a drain on the body's financial strength they can become contributors to its health through mission giving (see Titus 3:14; 1 John 3:17).

No Rotten Talk (4:29)

The Greek word which is translated *evil* (*sapros*) literally means *decayed*, *rotten*, or *spoiled*. It is used here to refer to filthy language, which is not appropriate for Christians. In ancient days, as in modern times, believers have always been tempted by those around them to be popular and use street language that is laced with sexual innuendo.

The writer says that speech is only to be used to build

up the church. *Edifying* is taken from the same Greek word that is used to describe the building up of the household of faith in 2:21; 4:12, 16. Christians are to use their words to benefit others by giving thanks to God, sharing the good news, preaching, teaching, and comforting one another (see Ephesians 5:4; Matthew 12:36-37; Colossians 3:8; 2 Timothy 2:14-17).

Do Not Grieve the Holy Spirit (4:30)

This verse could literally be translated, *Do not cause the Holy Spirit to suffer, in whom you have been sealed unto the day of redemption.* Sin causes God pain (Isaiah 63:10; Romans 8:26) and anger (Hebrews 10:29). For *sealed*, see Ephesians 1:13-14; for *redemption* see the discussion of Galatians 3:13 above.

Be Kindhearted (4:31-32)

Kindness is a Christian virtue and is a fruit of the Holy Spirit. See the discussion of Galatians 5:22. Forgiveness and love are given by Christians to each other because they have first learned them from Christ (Matthew 6:12, 14-15; 2 Corinthians 2:1-11; Colossians 3:12-13).

§ § § § § § §

The Message of Ephesians 4

§ The Spirit has called individuals to particular tasks in the church so that the whole church can grow and be built up in Christ's love.

§ The readers of the letter, who are Gentiles, are reminded that they are no longer trapped in their alienation from God or hardness of heart. They have been renewed by the Spirit and have put on Christ. Practical examples are given to illustrate how the new nature is manifested in concrete actions.

§ § § § § § §

Ephesians 5:1–6:17

Introduction to These Chapters

Chapters 5–6 are part of the second major section of Ephesians. The writer gives advice here concerning how to imitate God, how to live successfully in a Christian household, and how to be vigilant in the faith.

Be Imitators of God (5:1)

Christians are to model their behavior after God's; they are to mimic God. Because they are made in God's image (Genesis 1:27) and because they follow after Jesus Christ (1 Peter 2:21), they do not have to wonder how they should act. (See 1 Corinthians 11:1; 1 Thessalonians 1:6.)

For the Christian concept of being God's children, see Galatians 4:1-7.

Walk in Love (5:2)

The image of the Christian life as walking with God in love is used a number of times by this writer. See the discussion of Galatians 5:16 above.

Gave himself up for us, fragrant offering, and *sacrifice to God* is language the church uses to describe the significance of Christ's death on the cross. Christ freely made himself the sacrifice required by the Jewish law so that all those who believe in him could be free from the power of sin (Romans 3:23-26; 8:3; Galatians 2:20). The fragrant offering refers to the aroma of the offering which pleases God (Genesis 8:21; Exodus 29:18; 2 Corinthians 2:14-16; Philippians 4:18).

Put Away All Immorality (5:3-14)

The author has already indicated that immoral behavior is not appropriate for Christians (4:19, 22-24, 29). The best way for believers to act is out of joy and thanksgiving for what is being done for them in Christ (Colossians 3:5). In verse 5 he repeats the harsh judgment found in Galatians 5:21, that those who insist on behavior that is contrary to what God wants will not inherit the kingdom of God. Similar warnings are found throughout the Dead Sea Scrolls, where the people who lived at Qumran are warned that they must avoid all contamination by pagans and unbelieving Jews if they want to be God's children.

Empty words (verse 6) refers to the dangerous doctrines mentioned in 4:14 and the heresies that have caused this author to write the letter in the first place. *Sons of disobedience* (see 2:2) are those who are being ruled by sin, by rebellion against God (Romans 2:12-16). The *wrath of God* is God's judgment on the final day against all those who have not turned to God in Christ (John 3:36; 1 Thessalonians 1:10; Revelation 6:15-17).

In 5:7-14 the writer draws a sharp contrast once more between pagans and those Gentiles who have become Christians. He uses the religious language of light and darkness familiar in the ancient world. Those who do not believe in Christ are lost in the darkness of sin (4:18), whereas those who are in Christ are illuminated by the one who is himself the light of the world (John 8:12; 1 John 1:5-7; 2:8). The Jews who lived near the Dead Sea used similar language: They believed that humanity was divided between the children of light and the children of darkness, and they looked forward to one great battle when light would finally be victorious.

It is possible that, in these verses, the writer is also reacting to the influence of Gnostic ideas among his readers. Some Gnostic systems taught that the goal of salvation was to retrieve the divine spark or light in each human being so that all light could be returned to God, who was light. For this author it is not the god of a pagan religion who is light, but Jesus Christ who is truly the light of the whole cosmos.

The writer also believes that darkness is a sign of immorality. He builds in verses 11-14 on the common knowledge that during the night people commit all kinds of shameful acts, particularly the sexual sins mentioned in 4:19 and 22.

He closes the section with what appears to be a quotation of Old Testament Scripture in verse 14 (*therefore it is said*), but it is difficult to know for certain what text he has in mind. Perhaps it is a summary of several verses like Psalm 139:11-12, Isaiah 26:19; 60:1 or Jonah 1:6. He seems to combine two different ideas here: (1) The Christian should wake up and not behave like those who do immoral things in the darkness; and (2) the Christian should behave like those who have been raised from spiritual death (Ephesians 2:1-7), like those who have had life renewed in the Spirit (4:23-24).

Make the Most of the Time (5:15-17)

Before moving on to the rules of the Christian household, the writer summarizes the general principles of the Christian life. The Christian life is one of following Jesus and walking with God (see 2:1-2). Christians are to walk as wise persons, wisdom being a gift from God (1:9). They must remember that their minds and ways are not darkened (1:18; 4:17-18), but are illuminated by the light of Christ (5:7-14).

Believers must make every minute of every day count, making the most of the time. By this the writer may simply mean that because there is so much to do for God's work in the mission of the church, no time should be wasted (Matthew 9:37). Or, as is more likely, he may be warning his readers that they must be ready for Christ's return at any moment (Matthew 22:1-14; 24:3-14; 25:1-13).

Get High on the Spirit (5:18-20)

Christians are not to get drunk with wine (Proverbs 20:1; 23:31-35) but are to get high on the Spirit, being filled up with God's indwelling presence. The writer mentions the fullness of the Christian faith repeatedly (1:10, 23; 3:19; 4:10, 13). He may be contrasting Christian worship which consists of prayers and hymns with the drunken practices of those who worshiped the god of wine, Dionysus, or the services of some Greek mystery religions which ended with sexual orgies. If a person is full of the Holy Spirit, then all that is needed for stimulation is a spirit of joy and thanksgiving (5:4; Colossians 3:17; 1 Thessalonians 5:18).

Husbands and Wives (5:21-33)

Verse 21 introduces a section which is often called "the household code." A similar set of rules is found in Colossians 3:18–4:1, where instructions are given about proper Christian conduct within the family and the way slaves should be treated. It was common for writers of the first century to give moral advice to their readers and to include practical suggestions about everyday life.

Ephesians 5:21-33 is one of the most discussed and most misunderstood passages in the entire New Testament. In conservative Christian circles it is often taken strictly as a commandment about the order of power in the Christian household. Many Christians believe that the husband must be the head of the household in every way, that he must make all of the final decisions as if God had somehow endowed him with extraordinary wisdom far greater than that given to his wife or children. In many cases this means that he has complete control over all of the spiritual, emotional, and financial resources of the family, and other members of the family are nearly forced to become subservient to him.

Interpretations that insist that husbands must be the

controlling head of the house miss the significance of the writer's teaching in Ephesians 5. The key verse is 5:21, *Be subject to one another out of reverence for Christ*. Although it says in verses 22-24 that a wife must be subject to her husband, and that he is the head of the family, the whole section is subordinate to the first verse. Wives, according to this passage, are to be subject; they are to obey their husbands. But verse 21 indicates that husbands are also subject to their wives in Christ. There is a mutuality here which is often overlooked.

Frequently Ephesians 5 is cited as an example of the way the Bible makes women appear to be inferior to men. It cannot be be denied that biblical writers usually shared views commonly held in the ancient world that women were the weaker sex (1 Peter 3:7), that they should be kept in their place in the church (1 Corinthians 11:2-14; 14:34), and even that they were nothing more than property (see, for example, Numbers 5:11-31; Deuteronomy 22:13-21). Ephesians 5:21-33 goes far beyond these limited principles.

In many ways Ephesians 5 presents a rather revolutionary perspective about women. Even though this writer accepts the universally held belief in the ancient world that the man was the head of the household, he tells Christian husbands that they have additional burdens which make it impossible for them to mistreat their wives. The wife may be subject to the husband by custom, but spiritually he is also subject to Christ. He cannot do whatever he wants to her, since he must love her as much as Christ loved the church (5:25). Christ clearly loved the church with self-giving love, unbounded love, the kind of love that is willing to die for the other. What is more, the husband is ordered to love his wife as much as he loves his own body (5:28). Here the principle is the same as the second part of the Golden Rule (Matthew 22:39), *You shall love your neighbor as yourself*. The husband must now see that his wife is his Christian

144

neighbor and he must love her as one already loved by Jesus Christ.

In this chapter the writer continues to build on his understanding of the body of Christ (1:22-23; 2:14-22; 3:6; 4:4, 15-16). Just as Jews and Gentiles have been reconciled into one body in the church, and are all working and growing together in Christ's love, so the Christian family is also a metaphor for the church (compare 5:30 with 4:2-4). The one body formed by husband and wife (5:31) is similar to the one body made up of all Christians. In a sense, it would not make any difference if verse 22 read, "Husbands, be subject to your wives, as to the Lord," because the mutuality and love demanded would be entirely the same. In a Christian family, as in the church, all members are valued equally, and all members must function together if the family is to be what God intends it to be. There is really only one head of the family, and he is the same one who is the head of the church. Jesus Christ is the Lord of all. He is the one who upbuilds his church and all relationships grounded in him, through the self-giving love seen in his cross and resurrection.

Verse 26, the reference to the cleansing of the wife by the washing of water, is a play on words. It compares the prenuptial ceremonial bath of a bride as she prepares for her wedding day to the ceremony of baptism in which the new Christian is cleansed and made fit for being a member of Christ's body (see Acts 22:16; 1 Corinthians 6:11; Titus 3:5; 1 Peter 3:21). In 2 Corinthians 11:2 the apostle Paul somewhat similarly compares Jesus to the bridegroom ready to receive members of the Christian church as his "bride" (see Revelation 21:2).

The quotation in 5:31 is from Genesis 2:24. Jesus cites it as a basic spiritual principle of marriage in Matthew 19:5. (See 1 Corinthians 6:16.) Men and women are created to exist in complementary and co-equal ways. They are complementary physically, but their intimacy extends far beyond sexual compatibility. They can also have spiritual intimacy, as God intended from the beginning.)

In verse 33 the writer uses the word *mystery* to describe the relationship between a Christian wife and husband. The same word is used in 1:9 to describe the union of Jews and Gentiles in the church. The fear of the believer about God's wrath, or the fear of the wife toward her husband, are replaced by the self-giving love of Christ and the unity and fellowship which that love creates.

Children and Parents (6:1-4)

This piece of Christian advice is very similar to Colossians 3:20. Jews and Gentiles alike assumed that just as the husband had a right to expect his wife to obey him, his children should also obey (notice that the mother is not even mentioned in these verses). If any man could not control his children it was considered a mark of dishonor for him and his whole family (1 Timothy 3:4-5; see Proverbs 17:25).

The biblical quotation in verse 2 is from the Ten Commandments (Deuteronomy 5:16). The command attaches a promise that those who obey their parents will have long life. In the Old Testament the opposite was also the case. Sons who did not respect their parents could be put to death (Deuteronomy 21:18-21). Clearly, the writer expects that the children are part of the church and that they will hear his letter read because he addresses his warning directly to them.

In verse 4 he also directs advice to the fathers, which goes beyond admonitions given in the Old Testament. Even though discipline is necessary in the family (Proverbs 13:24; 29:17), the Christian father must love his children in the Lord and must extend the love and teaching of Christ to those under his care.

Slaves and Masters (6:5-9)

As in Colossians 3:22–4:1, advice is given to masters about the way they should treat their slaves. Although slavery was the most cruel institution imaginable, Christians did not resist it in the first century or for many centuries after that, and the writer clearly expects that many of his readers will be slave owners. In Philemon, the apostle demonstrates a charitable attitude toward the way a slave should be treated. However, it is also clear that Paul believes the rule of secular law is that a slave never has a right to emancipate himself.

The slave is subject to the master as though to Christ himself (6:5). He or she is to work willingly, as if serving the Lord, and must give more than eye-service (Colossians 3:22) or face time. Although the language is similar to that addressed to the Christian wife (5:22), it lacks the mutuality of the marriage bonds. The master might also be subject to Christ, but he is not subject to the slave (5:21). Nevertheless, the writer goes beyond what was normally expected of slave owners in the ancient world, even benevolent ones, and requires that the master avoid any hint of unnecessary punishment or cruelty. The principle upon which this good spirit is based is the love of Christ. Slave owners and slaves are both servants (6:7; the Greek root literally means *slave*) of Christ and both are subject to him (Colossians 4:1). The indication here is that slaves were also members of the church and they had to be given special consideration since they were also members of the one body of Christ (Galatians 3:28; Philemon 16).

With 6:9 the writer concludes his discussion of the Christian household begun in 2:19. All relationships, whether religious, political, economic, or personal, are changed by the presence of Jesus Christ. Christ is the head of all households, and he does not treat members of the church differently because of sex, social status, or wealth.

Put On the Whole Armor of God (6:10-17)

In 6:10-17 the writer completes his long section of Christian advice by reminding his readers that they are involved in a spiritual fight to the finish. (The use of military metaphors is common in the New Testament. See the discussions of Ephesians 4:8, 12; Galatians 2:12; 5:1, 13-15, 20, 25.) The battle is against the divine beings in the higher heavens, principalities, powers, aions, dominions, even the devil himself. Christ, through his victory on the cross, has overcome all of these evil forces. But the Christian must remain vigilant, on guard, and alert, for there are skirmishes to be fought and engagements still to be won or lost.

The Christian, therefore, is given the weapons and defensive armaments needed to insure final victory. *Be strong* (verse 10) is a little misleading, and seems to present the picture of a soldier pulling himself by his own boot straps. Rather, it means *be strengthened*, and points to the fact that the believer gets strength from God, through the Holy Spirit (3:16).

Armor is mentioned in verses 11 and 13. The description that follows lists almost all of the pieces of equipment (see 4:12, *equipment of the saints*) which a well-outfitted Roman soldier would need to fight. The Roman historian Polybius lists the shield, the breastplate, leg coverings, helmet, sword, and two javelins. The picture that the writer of Ephesians draws in verse 13 is one of a soldier who is able to stand his ground without giving up an inch. The image of the soldier ready to fight for spiritual truth and justice is also known in the Old Testament (Isaiah 59:17) and the Apocrypha (Wisdom 5:17-20). It appears in the New Testament in several places (2 Corinthians 6:7; 10:3-4; 1 Thessalonians 5:8).

Christian soldiers are fighting for spiritual victories, not to obtain prestige, territory, wealth, or power. Their weapons are qualities that come from the Holy Spirit. Their battle is for the peace (6:15) that the reconciling presence of Christ brings.

Christian soldiers are outfitted defensively and offensively from foot to head. The combat boot is made up of the equipment of peace mentioned in Isaiah 52:7. Christians are disciplined to march only for peace and justice and to bring good news to the oppressed. They are evangelists and preachers (Romans 10:15). Their thighs are protected by truth, the ultimate truth in Christ Jesus (see Ephesians 4:21). The breastplate, which was made of metal and leather and protected the chest and throat, is righteousness for the Christian, or what is called *justification* or *justice* elsewhere in the New Testament (Galatians 2:21; 3:6, 21). The shield of faith is compared to the manueverable defensive weapon which the soldiers held in their hands. Often the shield was dipped in water before a battle, and when the enemy fired burning arrows they could easily be deflected or put out by the shields. In the battle for the spirits of human beings the flaming darts are the wiles or the tricks of the devil (see 2 Timothy 2:26). Faith in Jesus Christ is the force that enables the Christian to be successful in the cosmic battle with evil. The helmet of salvation is probably a reference to Isaiah 59:17 (see 1 Thessalonians 5:8).

The only offensive weapon the Christian needs is the the sword of the Spirit, which is the word of God. The writer's thinking here is similar to Hebrews 4:12, where it says that *the word of God is living and active, sharper than any two-edged sword, piercing to the division of soul and spirit, of joints and marrow.* The word of God is God's creative power. No one can resist its force for truth, and it is the ultimate weapon against evil (John 1:1-5).

§ § § § § § §

The Message of Ephesians 5–6

§ Christians must be imitators of Christ, and be grounded in sacrificial love. They should no longer associate with those who are lost in the darkness of sin, but should conduct themselves as children illuminated by the light of Christ.

§ The writer gives advice on running a household—how husbands and wives should interact, how fathers should treat children, and how masters should treat slaves. All advice is centered in the love of Christ, in the fellowship of the household of faith.

§ Christians are also warned to be vigilant in their faith. Even though Christ will be victorious over all spiritual enemies, important battles remain to be fought, and believers are given special equipment of faith so they may stand fast.

§ § § § § § §

PART NINETEEN **Ephesians 6:18-24**

Introduction to These Verses

In the last seven verses the writer urges his readers to remain alert and prepared for the continuing spiritual battle. They must pray in the Spirit since the Spirit is the one who counsels and strengthens them in all ways. They must also pray for other believers who need God's help. The writer is in special need himself since he is in prison, a representative of Christ even to those who are his captors.

Some Prayers to Offer (6:18-20)

In his final thoughts, the writer of Ephesians visualizes his readers as constantly being on military alert (verse 18). They are always ready to pray for others and proclaim the truth about Jesus Christ.

This section is very similar to Colossians 4:2-7, so much so that many biblical scholars are convinced that this part of Ephesians was copied from the last verses of Colossians. In both letters the readers are directed to pray at all times. Prayer is the way in which Christians keep in touch with the commander-in-chief during spiritual warfare; it is the way orders for mission are communicated. Prayer is also the method God uses to strengthen believers in the inner person (3:16). Praying in the Spirit indicates that it is God's Holy Spirit who brings power, comfort, and consolation, and lives within those who believe in Christ (1:13-14; 2:22; John 14:15-17, 25-26).

The Spirit is even the one who prays for us when we

do not know what to say (Mark 13:11; Romans 8:26). The writer urges Christians to be as close to God as they can, since they will need God's power and love for the battles that are surely coming. The command to pray at all times is a common one throughout the New Testament (1 Thessalonians 5:17; 1 Timothy 2:1; 2 Timothy 1:3).

Keep alert is also a common scriptural directive. Christians must not only be ready for spiritual battle at any time, but must also be prepared for Christ's return and the coming day of the Lord (Mark 13; Luke 21:36).

One of the duties of Christians is to engage in intercessory prayer for other Christians. This writer wants his readers to lift up other believers before God so that they may be strengthened in their ministries and personal lives. Those who have been through difficult times know how much support they receive when they know that others are praying for them. The writer also needs this support because he is an ambassador in chains (see 3:1; 4:1).

The Greek verb which he uses for *ambassador* here is the same word from which we get our words *elder*, *presbyter* and *presbyterian*. The same word is used in 2 Corinthians 5:20. A presbyter was an elder statesman or a member of the city council who was selected for his wisdom. The writer is in chains, not because he is guilty of a crime or because he is incompetent, but because he has been selected by God to represent Christ and to speak boldly and deliver the message of the mystery of the gospel (see 3:8-9).

Tychicus Brings This Letter (6:21-22)

The note about the person who is delivering this letter, Tychicus, is almost identical to the comment in Colossians 4:7. If, as is likely, the apostle Paul did not write Ephesians, the reference to Tychicus has no historical value. It is merely a copying of what was written to the Colossian congregation. Paul's letters often indicate that others served him as secretaries (see Galatians 6:11) and carried news about him and other churches.

Benediction (6:23-24)

The letter ends with almost the same words with which it begins (1:2). The writer's message concludes with a prayer for spiritual peace in the midst of a battle with evil spiritual forces, faith in a world that constantly doubts the power of God, and reliance on the free gift of God (grace) when most people around him are selfish and unforgiving. This peace, inner strength, and knowledge of forgiveness only come from one source; it is the eternal (undying) love of Jesus Christ that binds all living things into the loving purpose of God (1:4-5, 15; 2:4; 4:2, 15, 16; 5:2). Therefore, being rooted and grounded in love, we may have the power to comprehend what is the breadth and length and height and depth, and to know the love of Christ which surpasses knowledge, so that we may all be filled with the fullness of God.

§ § § § § § §

The Message of Ephesians 6:18-24

§ The letter closes with words nearly identical to the letter's beginning: Peace, faith, and God's forgiveness in Christ are all realized in the eternal, self-giving love of Jesus Christ.

§ § § § § § §

Glossary of Terms

Abba: The Aramaic term term for *father* used by Paul.

Antioch: A city located in northern Syria which Paul often visited.

Aramaic: A language similar to Hebrew spoken in Palestine in the first century A.D.

Amen: A Hebrew word used to end prayers which means *Be it so!*

Apostle: One who is sent by God. A special title of authority and power in the early church.

Arabia: A name for two different places, one in Syria, east of Damascus, and another in the desert region near Egypt where the Ten Commandments were given.

Barnabas: An apostle who went with Paul on his first missionary journey.

Cephas: The Aramaic name for the apostle Peter. It means *rock.*

Circumcision: A surgical act of cutting back the foreskin of the penis. Jews regarded it as a sign from God that they were the people of the covenant.

Covenant: The contract or promise God first gave to Abraham in Genesis 12:1-3. It was a sign that the Jews were God's special people (Jeremiah 31).

Custodian: A person, often a slave, who was responsible for taking children to school and making sure that they were educated and brought up correctly.

Dividing Wall: A fence, railing, or hedge used for protection. In Ephesians it refers to the wall in the Jerusalem Temple that divided the Gentiles from the Jews.

Doxology: A prayer that praises God.

Ephesus: A city located on the western coast of what is now Turkey.

Galatia: An area somewhere in central or northern Asia Minor (Turkey).

Gentiles: A word used by Jews to describe all non-Jews.

Glory: God's majesty. Literally it refers to one's "weight" or "value".

Gnostic: A person who believed in Gnosticism.

Gnosticism: Philosophical systems and religions that placed great emphasis on special knowledge (*gnosis*) that only their members possessed. Gnostics often believed in complex systems of heavenly levels and divine beings who populated them.

Grace: The gift of God's love and forgiveness through Jesus Christ.

James: The brother of Jesus who was a leader of the Jerusalem church after Jesus' ascension.

John: An apostle who often traveled with Peter. He was one of Jesus' original disciples.

Justification: Paul's concept of being forgiven without having to keep all of the commandments of the law. The Christian is "put right" with God through faith alone, not by anything that is done or not done.

Law: The law can refer to several different things: the Ten Commandments; the large body of Jewish legal ordinances and customs called the Torah; the natural order of things; God's rule for living; secular law.

Mount Sinai: A mountain in the Arabian peninsula where Moses received the Ten Commandments. Also called Mount Horeb in the Old Testament.

Mystery: The secret of God's plan for Jews and Gentiles in Christ. The New Testament writers believed that it was uncovered for the first time through Jesus' life, death, and resurrection. In the ancient world other religious groups believed that they were the only ones who were initiated into God's secrets and thus their belief systems were often called "mystery religions."

Redemption: The act of exchanging one thing for something else. In the Bible as a whole the term refers to God's payment for the high cost of sin. In the New Testament the word refers to the sacrifice of Christ and the way it brings about God's forgiveness.

Sin: Rebellion or hostility directed toward God; literally "missing the mark."

Guide to Pronunciation

Abba: AH-bah
Antioch: AN-tee-ahk
Arabia: Ah-RAY-be-ah
Cephas: SEE-phus
Cilicia: Sih-LIH-shuh
Circumcision: SUR-kum-sih-zhun
Damascus: Duh-MAS-kuhs
Ephesus: EF-uh-sus
Exhortation: Ex-or-TAY-shun
Galatia: Gah-LAY-shuh
Gentile: JEN-tile
Gnostic: NOSS-tik
Gnosticism: NOSS-tih-siz-um
Hagar: HAY-gahr
Isaac: EYE-zik
Judaism: JUDE-ah-iz-um
Judea: Joo-DEE-ah
Sinai: SIGH-nigh
Titus: TIE-tus
Tychicus: TIK-ih-kus

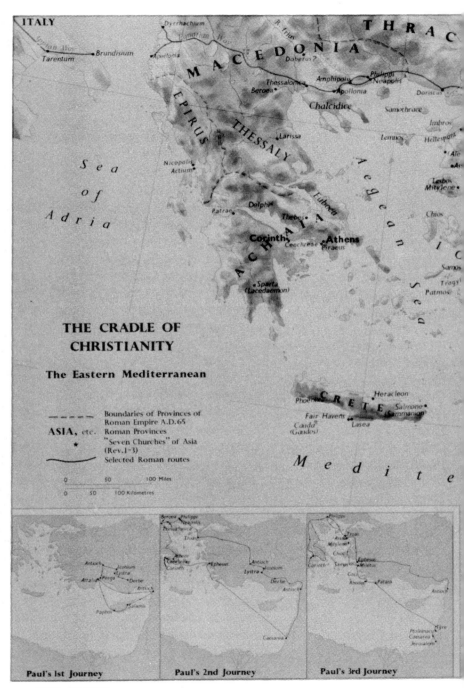

ITALY

Dyrrachium

THRAC

M A C E D O N I A

Egnatian Way
Tarentum • *Brundisium*
Apollonia
Doberus?

EPIRUS

THESSALY

Thessalonica
Beroea •
Amphipolis
Apollonia
Philippi • *Neapolis*
Samothrace
Doriscus

Chalcidice

Imbros

Larissa

Lemnos
Hellespont

A e g e a n

Nicopolis
Actium

Lesbos
Mytilene •

Patrae
Delphi
Euboea
Thebes

Chios

Corinth
Cenchreae
Athens
Piraeus

Samos
Trogy
Patmos

A C H A I A

• *Sparta*
(Lacedaemon)

THE CRADLE OF
CHRISTIANITY

The Eastern Mediterranean

Heracleon
Phoenix
C R E T E
Salmone
Cammania
Fair Havens
Cauda •
(Gaudos)
Lasea

– – – – – Boundaries of Provinces of
Roman Empire A.D. 65
ASIA, etc. Roman Provinces
★ "Seven Churches" of Asia
(Rev.1–3)
———— Selected Roman routes

M e d i t e r

0   50   100 Miles
0   50   100 Kilometres

Paul's 1st Journey

Antioch
Iconium
Lystra
Attalia *Perga* • *Derbe*
• *Antioch*
Paphos *Salamis*

Paul's 2nd Journey

Beroea *Philippi*
Amphipolis
Thessalonica
Troas
Athens
Ephesus
Cenchreae *Antioch*
Corinth
Lystra *Iconium*
Derbe
• *Antioch*
Caesarea •

Paul's 3rd Journey

Philippi
Assos
Mytilene
Chios
Corinth *Samos*
Ephesus
Miletus
Cos
Rhodes • *Patara*
• *Antioch*
Ptolemais
Tyre
Caesarea
Jerusalem

ASIA MINOR

From the *Oxford Bible Atlas*, Third Edition

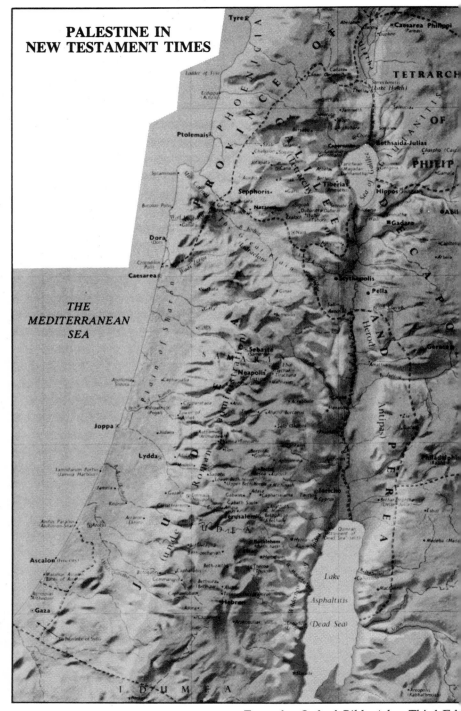

PALESTINE IN
NEW TESTAMENT TIMES

THE
MEDITERRANEAN
SEA

From the *Oxford Bible Atlas*, Third Ed